ВЕЛИ М ПАНТЕЛЕИМОНЪ

М СЕРГІЙ

М ВАКХЪ

М ФЛОРЪ

М ЛАVРЪ

СЩЕННО М СVМЕШНЪ

СЩЕННО М АНТVП

MONASTERIES

Places of spirituality and seclusion around the world

Markus Hattstein

MONASTERIES

Places of spirituality and seclusion worldwide

PaRragon

Bath · New York · Singapore · Hong Kong · Cologne · Delhi
Melbourne · Amsterdam · Johannesburg · Auckland · Shenzhen

CONTENTS

Introduction

Monasteries have always been places of retreat, quiet contemplation, and prayer (Latin: *claustrum*, a place of seclusion). They have also been centers of learning, colonization and civilization, healing and music, Church politics and religious conflict, and above all art and architecture—and remain so today.

Based on examples drawn from different art-historical and architectural periods, this book takes its readers on a journey into the world of the monastery. Both historically significant and less well-known (but nevertheless architecturally appealing) monasteries are examined in word and image. This book comprises three parts, the main part of which focuses on the monasteries of western and central Europe and America. The second part discusses the multifaceted world of

the Orthodox monastery in eastern Europe and the Middle East. The later chapters look at the monasteries of Hinduism, Buddhism, Jainism, Daoism, and Islam.

The beginnings—desert hermits and monasteries

Christianity's earliest monks were hermits who withdrew to the desert in order to devote their lives to prayer. Choosing as their abodes rock caves or tombs, they often had themselves immured within, and relied on supporters to provide them with food. Over time, hermits' retreats, in close proximity to one another, developed into the first monastic communities. These consisted of a group of simple buildings

Monastery on the Hebridean island of Iona (Scotland), the spiritual center of Hiberno-Scottish monasticism and its evangelization of the continent of Europe.

enclosed by walls. The ascetic life of these highly disciplined communities, which were governed by an abbot, placed an emphasis on equality and lack of possessions. In general, the monks or nuns came together only for meals and communal prayers in the monastery church, spending the rest of their time in individual cells—such as the stone "beehive" huts of the Hiberno-Scottish monks, numbers of which still survive. The monastic fathers drew up extremely strict and austere codes by which the monks were expected to live. The first such "rule" was that of the Egyptian monk Pachomius (c. 292–346), which formed the basis for later codes adopted by monasteries throughout the West, such as the Rule of St. Columbanus of Luxeuil (540–615).

St. Benedict of Nursia and the Benedictine order

St. Benedict of Nursia (480–547) played a decisive role in the development of Western monasticism. His rule, based on the motto *ora et labora* (prayer and work), stresses the Benedictine objective of a communal life founded on manual work and contemplative prayer. Monasteries now began to develop into self-sufficient, village-like complexes whose monks labored in workshops, farmed the land, and reared livestock. The monasteries embarked on a tremendous program of civilizing measures. As well as cultivating the land, they also cultivated the mind, and their monastery schools and scriptoria made them pillars of Western learning. As a result of privileges and endowments from powerful feudal lords, monastery churches soon numbered among the most important places of worship within a given region. In the 10th and 11th centuries, the Cluny reforms eventually gave monasteries an even greater degree of independence from the sovereign.

From an architectural point of view, the most glorious period of church and monastery building occurred during the Romanesque and Gothic eras. The sturdy-looking structures of the Romanesque age were succeeded by the slender, graceful, and soaring forms (the "reaching heavenward") of the Gothic age, during which filigree

The monastic father and hermit St. Anthony the Great (251–356), whose life served the earliest monastic communities as a model (Matthias Grünewald, figure study for the Isenheim Altarpiece, c. 1512/16).

*Above left: wall paintings above the tomb of monastic father St. Anthony in the **monastery of St. Anthony in the desert near Zafrana** (Egypt).*

*Above right: St. Benedict of Nursia supervises the construction of 12 Benedictine abbeys (fresco in the cloister of the **abbey of Monte Oliveto Maggiore**, 16th century). The founding of new houses by monks from the mother monasteries proceeded swiftly and efficiently.*

*Opposite page: Late Gothic portal of the church of the **Dominican monastery of Santa Maria da Vitória in Batalha** (Portugal), founded in 1385.*

decoration in the form of buttresses, doors, and the tracery of pointed windows reached its apex.

Monasteries of the reform orders

A number of reform orders emerged in reaction to the ambitious monastery buildings and wealth of the Benedictine order. In the 12th century, the Cistercians returned to the original ideals of St. Benedict, building their monasteries on desolate marshes in a simple and functional style that dispensed with any decoration. Their colonization efforts, which involved great privation, and their strict organization into parent and dependent monasteries, ensured the swift diffusion of the order throughout Europe. In terms of rules and architecture, other orders—such as the Carthusians, Carmelites, and later Trappists—returned to the very roots of monasticism, seeking to combine forms of communal religious life with eremitism.

The mendicant Franciscans and Dominicans had a big impact on monastic life. Both of these orders dedicated themselves to preaching, the spiritual welfare of the people, and care for the poor, and therefore built their monasteries not behind high walls but in the centers of towns and cities,

where they blended with the surrounding architecture. In the "poverty controversy" of the 13th century, the radical section of the Franciscan order came out strongly against the secular power and wealth of the Church and the monasteries, while the Dominicans busied themselves with doctrine and the inquisition against "heretics" and "deviants."

Monasteries during the Reformation and Counter-Reformation

These developments were harbingers of the Reformation that transformed the Church in central Europe in the 16th century. The Protestant rulers dissolved the monasteries and confiscated their property. Numerous monasteries were destroyed or plundered by peasants and radical iconoclasts as despised symbols of secular temporal power, while others were laid to waste during the wars of religion.

During the Counter-Reformation, monastic life was revived by the Catholic Church. The Jesuit order, which was organized along military lines, established its churches and monasteries in university towns and centers of religious conflict. Like the Capuchins, a reform branch of the Franciscan order, the Jesuits devoted themselves to the

*Baroque splendor: in 1744 Franz Martin Kuen completed an enormous ceiling fresco in the library of the **Benedictine monastery of Wiblingen in Ulm**. Founded in 1093, the monastery was completely remodeled in the Baroque style from 1714 onwards.*

spiritual welfare of the people, seeking proximity to the lay congregations. At the same time, the orders embarked on a new sphere of activity (from an architectural perspective, too) in the form of the conversion and colonization of the "New World," and Latin America in particular.

From the Baroque to the present

The Renaissance love of detailed ornament had already set in motion a departure from simple and functional monastery architecture. This process was consummated during the Baroque era. From the 17th century onward, the exuberant wealth and power of the "Church triumphant"—as whose representatives the monasteries saw themselves—gave rise to grandiose ostentation on the part of the monasteries. Nearly all the abbeys dating from the early years were refurbished in the Baroque style or replaced by Baroque structures with immense churches and libraries dominated by vast paintings and ceiling frescoes.

During the 19th century there was a movement away from Baroque magnificence. Monastic buildings once again became simpler, and at the same time took on a

romanticizing character: neo-Romanesque and neo-Gothic styles harked back to the medieval golden age of the monasteries and borrowed from the earlier age in their detail. Monastic architecture of the 20th century, on the other hand, embraced a wide variety of influences. In addition to a more conventional style of architecture and the reutilization of existing buildings for different purposes, modern styles were adopted that combined functionality with aesthetics and a contemplative quality.

Monasteries of the Orthodox churches

The legacy of the desert fathers also flowed into the great monastic tradition of the Orthodox churches. In terms of organization and architectural styles, elements of the early years were adopted by the monasteries of the Syrian, Egyptian, Coptic, and Ethiopian Orthodox churches in particular. In the 6th century, the Greek Orthodox monasteries started to thrive under the Byzantine Empire, which they provided with spiritual support in a number of respects. Large monastic communities developed in Greece, with the monasteries of Metéora and the monastic republic of Mount Athos, but also in the Balkan lands of present-day Bulgaria, Serbia, and Romania.

With the Ottoman conquest of Constantinople in 1453, leadership of the Eastern Church eventually passed to Russia. The czars supported the Russian and Ukrainian monasteries, which developed into large walled settlements with magnificently appointed monastery cathedrals; these held sway over thousands of serfs in hundreds of surrounding villages. Like the Byzantine Church, the Russian Orthodox Church remained the State Church for a long time. Many of its important monasteries were rebuilt in the style of the (Russian) Baroque in the 17th and 18th centuries.

Hindu, Buddhist, Jain, Daoist, and Islamic monasteries

Monasteries and various forms of monasticism as an expression of temporary or lifelong withdrawal from the agitation of everyday life—in favor of prayer, contemplation, study, and good works—are not exclusive to Christianity. In Hinduism, monasteries (*matha*) continue today to be serviced by the Brahmin, perpetuating their individual traditions of the veneration of deities Vishnu and Shiva, while ashrams are monastery-like centers for the practice of meditation. During the early period (from the 5th century BC onwards), Buddhism and Jainism were overwhelmingly monastic, and large monastery complexes were erected. As the "land of monasteries," Tibet occupies a special position in the history of Buddhism, although Southeast Asia, with its *wats*, and Japan, with its Zen Buddhism, possess important monastic traditions of their own. Daoism, in China, was also responsible for the construction of striking monastery complexes. Finally, monastic life has played an important part in Islam with the *ribats* of warrior monks in the frontier regions of the Muslim world and the *tekkes* built by the mystical Sufi orders.

*Interior of the temple hall of the **Buddhist (Tibetan Lamaist) monastery of Tamang** in northeast India (state of Arunachal Pradash).*

The Monasteries of Western Christendom

The First Monasteries in the West

Benedict of Nursia (480–547) founded his first monastery in 529 at the top of a rocky outcrop known as Monte Cassino. This mother monastery of the Benedictine order has been destroyed repeatedly over the course of time: by the Lombards in 577 (rebuilt in 717), by the Saracens in 883, by an earthquake in 1349, by Napoleon's troops (severely damaged) in 1799, and most recently by the Allied bombardment of February 1944.

Among the abbey's most important features are its cloisters. The entrance cloister was built on the site of a chapel of St. Martin erected by St. Benedict. This gives onto another cloister, dating from 1512, thought to have been built by the Renaissance artist and architect Donato Bramante, and a courtyard at whose center stands an octagonal well. From here a flight of steps leads to another cloister, which contains statues of the monastery's benefactors. Like other parts of the complex, the abbey church was rebuilt in the Baroque style during the 17th and 18th centuries. In 1944 it was completely destroyed, along with its frescoes and paintings, but was rebuilt in the old style after the war.

Monastic apparel and daily routine as prescribed by St. Benedict of Nursia

Clothing and possessions:
2 tunics: undergarment of wool or linen with short sleeves, also serving as nightwear
2 cucullae: overgarment (cowl) with hood and long sleeves
1 scapular: worn over the tunic, a fabric tabard hanging low over chest and back
1 bracile: a fabric or leather girdle
2 pairs of shoes: sandals (sometimes just foot cloths) for summer; wooden shoes for winter
Bedding, knife, needle, handkerchief, stylus, and writing tablet

Daily prayers:
01:00: Vigils or Nocturns: psalms, lessons, canticles, and hymn *Te Deum Laudamus* interspersed with antiphons
Between 02:00 and 05:00 (depending on season): Lauds or Matins: psalms 66 and 50, two variable psalms and psalms 148–50
05:00/06:00: Prime: hymn and psalms
09:00: Terce: hymn and psalms
12:00: Sext: hymn and psalms
15:00: None: hymn and psalms
17:00/18:00: Vespers: hymn and psalms
Between 18:00 and 21:00: Compline: hymn and psalms

Working hours of the monks:
8 hours in summer; 6–7 hours in winter

Above left: the **abbey of Monte Cassino** *was one of the earliest and most highly respected places of learning during the Middle Ages. It reached its theological apogee in the 11th century, during the course of which two of its abbots were enthroned as pope.*

Above right: the crypt at **Monte Cassino** *is the only part of the abbey that survived destruction in 1944. It is the resting place of St. Benedict of Nursia, who died at the abbey in 547.*

Left: the spacious inner courtyard. At its peak, more than 200 monks lived at the abbey.

*View of the nave (completed 1030) of the **abbey church of St. Peter and St. Paul at Romainmôtier**, looking west. The round columns have cushion capitals.*

Romainmôtier

Romainmôtier, Switzerland's oldest monastery, was founded in 450 by the French monk St. Romain (Romanus of Condat) and rebuilt in 632 following its destruction by the Alemanni. Its monks initially followed the Rule of St. Columbanus but adopted the Rule of St. Benedict at the pope's instigation in 753 and became a dependent priory of the reform abbey of Cluny in 928/9.

The abbey church, constructed between 990 and 1030, is one of the oldest Romanesque structures in Switzerland. It is built on a cruciform ground plan with a nave and two side aisles, a transept, and a crossing tower that was given a slender spire in the 15th century. The apses were replaced

by Gothic chapels in the 14th/15th centuries. It contains a number of important tombs as well as richly carved choir stalls. The abbey was dissolved during the Reformation (1536) and its buildings partly demolished.

Apart from St. Benedict of Nursia, the most important founder of monasteries in the West during the early Christian period was the Irish monk St. Columbanus of Luxeuil (540–615), who founded the abbey of Luxeuil in Burgundy in 590. St. Columbanus composed his own monastic rule, which was stricter and placed a greater emphasis on penance and asceticism than that of St. Benedict. As a strict preacher of morals, St. Columbanus fell into conflict with the Merovingian kings and was banished to Italy, where he founded the abbey of San

*Left: this view of the **monastery complex at Romainmôtier** shows the abbey church with its characteristic needle spire.*

*Below: the ruins of **Jumièges Abbey**, which for a long time was an important center of monastic and spiritual life in the western Frankish Empire. Tassilo III, the deposed last duke of Bavaria, was banished here by Charlemagne in 788.*

Colombano in Bobbio, Piacenza. He subsequently died there, three years later.

One of the most important abbeys in the Merovingian Empire was that of Jumièges, founded by St. Philibert (a nobleman who renounced court life) in 645. After having been burned down by the Vikings in 841, Jumièges Abbey was reoccupied by the Benedictine order. The abbey church with twin-towered west front, square crossing tower, arcading, and a groin vault was built in the mid-11th century and was instrumental in establishing a new style in Normandy. Important chronicles and translations of classical works of philosophy were produced at Jumièges, which was eventually laid to waste in 1562 during the French Wars of Religion.

Hiberno-Scottish Monasteries

*Opposite page: the ruins of **Lindisfarne Abbey**, where the celebrated "Lindisfarne Gospels," which testify to the sophistication of Celtic book art, originated. Abandoned in 875, the monastery was reoccupied by Benedictine monks in 1082. It was dissolved by the English Crown in 1539.*

From around 500, the early monasteries of Britain and Ireland, which were self-governing and followed their own monastic rules, developed into centers of Christianization of a peculiarly Celtic character. Sponsored by the regional kings of Britain and Ireland, these monasteries, many of which were also episcopal seats, developed into large settlements comprising complexes of stone and wooden buildings that housed not just monks but craftsmen too. Book art was practiced and many literary jewels produced in monasteries that had in many cases become refuges of Celtic self-assertion.

In 635 St. Aidan, a monk from the Scottish island of Iona, founded Lindisfarne Abbey on an island off the coast of Northumbria. He was succeeded as abbot by St. Cuthbert and subsequently St. Eadfrith. The cult of these saints made Lindisfarne a major place of pilgrimage, but continual attacks by the Vikings forced the monks to abandon the monastery and flee with the relics of their saints in 875. The episcopal seat was transferred to Durham.

Irish monks as missionaries in Europe

The Church in Britain and Ireland was dominated by Hiberno-Scottish monks. It asserted its Celtic independence through a flat hierarchical structure, autonomous bishops and abbots, its own rites of ordination, baptism, monastic tonsure, and by setting its own date for Easter. The monks often lived in stone "beehive" huts such as those on the islands of Iona and Lindisfarne.

Another peculiarity of Hiberno-Scottish monasticism were the wandering Irish bishops who undertook missionary work among the pagan peoples. One example is St. Columbanus of Luxeuil, who established his own "Rule." Another was St. Kilian, who was killed with his companions Totnan and Colman in Würzburg in 689. The conflict with central papal authority was ended by St. Boniface in the 8th century, when he brought the monasteries of the Frankish Empire under the control of Rome and the Benedictine order.

*Right: during the early days of Celtic Christianity, monks came together to lead an ascetic, eremitic existence incorporating elements of communal living. As here on the remote Irish island of **Skellig Michael**, the monks lived adjacent to one another in stone "beehive" huts grouped around a central chapel.*

*Above: the walled "Anchorite Chapel" at **Fore Abbey** contains a monastic cell in which Ireland's last hermit, one Patrick Beglan, lived until 1616.*

*Right: the solid-looking stone chapel of **Glendalough Abbey**, dedicated to St. Kevin and dating from the 11th century, is known as "St. Kevin's Kitchen" because of its chimney-like tower.*

In Ireland the monastery of Clonmacnoise by the River Shannon (County Offaly) was founded by the Irish monk and wandering bishop St. Ciarán from the Aran Islands, and a first church built in 545. Endowments and the abbey's good location on trading routes enabled new churches and other buildings to be almost constantly added.

At Clonmacnoise many of the peculiar features of the early Irish monasteries have been preserved, including a sturdy round tower of stone (in which relics and the abbey treasures could be brought to safety during times of danger), completed in 1124, and high crosses with stone "sun" rings (symbols of Celtic Christianity), the oldest of the four dating from around 800.

Another important monastic center was Glendalough Abbey, founded by St. Kevin as a place of retreat in the 6th century. Here too a round tower (erected around 1066) and high cross (St. Kevin's Cross) have survived, as has an early chapel known as "St. Kevin's Kitchen."

Fore Abbey, among the lakes of County Westmeath, was founded by St. Fechin in 630. By 665 the abbey

was already home to 300 monks and the complex was continually expanded, not least through the addition of two round towers (which survive as ruins). A total of 18 high crosses were also erected in Fore and the surrounding area. In around 1200 a Benedictine priory was constructed next to the old complex.

At the monastery founded in 588 on the remote island of Skellig Michael off the southwest coast of Ireland, the monks lived in six small stone houses with gardens clustered around a chapel dedicated to St. Michael.

The raid on Lindisfarne in 793 marked the beginning of attacks on the Hiberno-Scottish monasteries by Vikings, who were succeeded in Ireland by the Normans, following the Norman conquest of England in 1066. Fore Abbey had been burned down 12 times by 1169. Clonmacnoise was destroyed on a number of occasions and Skellig Michael was attacked in 823. Most of the monasteries were dissolved by the English Crown in 1539; the remaining Irish houses were destroyed as spiritual centers of national consciousness by Oliver Cromwell in the 17th century.

*Above: surviving elements of the extensive monastic site at **Clonmacnoise** include a round tower (a characteristic feature of many Irish monasteries) and cruciform gravestones incorporating a "sun" ring, a traditional symbol of Celtic Christianity.*

*Left: the ruins of the **monastery of Clonmacnoise**, surrounded by standing stone memorial slabs. The monastery fell into decline after a series of attacks by the Anglo-Normans around 1200. It was ultimately laid to waste by English troops in the 17th century.*

Benedictine Abbeys in the Frankish Empire

St. Peter's Abbey in Salzburg. In the early 17th century (starting in 1605) the abbey church was remodeled in the Renaissance style, and from 1756 onwards the entire complex was refurbished in keeping with Baroque taste. A number of additional chapels were also built at this time. Salzburg Cathedral can be seen in the background to the right.

Starting with the baptism in 498 of Clovis I (reigned 482–511), the Frankish kings began sponsoring the foundation of monasteries as centers of learning and Christianization. In terms of monastic rule, the first houses to be founded, mostly by Hiberno-Scottish monks, adopted a combination of the work precepts of St. Benedict of Nursia (*ora et labora*: pray and work) and the stricter Rule of St. Columbanus of Luxeuil. During the fratricidal wars between the Merovingian kings who controlled different parts of the realm, the monasteries competed for privileges and independence, but all worked hard at cultivating the land through agriculture and fish-farming.

St. Peter's Abbey in Salzburg, the oldest surviving monastery in the German-speaking lands, was founded in 696 by St. Rupert, the first bishop of Salzburg, and for some 300 years the (arch)bishops of Salzburg also served as abbots of St. Peter's. It was St. Rupert who built the first abbey church, which was replaced by the present building in the 12th century. The mighty church tower was raised even higher in 1400.

In the French part of the Frankish Empire, the abbey of St. Germain d'Auxerre, founded by Bishop Germanus of Auxerre after 418, was to attain particular importance. The abbey's simple chapel contained the relics of the highly revered martyr St. Maurice (died 290) and his companions of the Theban Legion. In 448 Germanus was in turn buried there.

After 511, Clovis's consort Clotilde had the chapel converted into a basilica and the abbey enjoyed the special protection of the Frankish ruler. Instances of miraculous healing at the saints' tombs made the church a place of pilgrimage, and led in the 9th century to the construction of a new basilica over 330 feet (100 m) in length. During the 11th and 12th centuries the complex was comprehensively renovated and a double-towered façade added, of which only the south tower survives. A Gothic rebuilding of the church in the 13th and 14th centuries remained unfinished. Following the French Revolution, the abbey buildings were transformed into a hospital.

*Left: the crypt of **St. Germain d'Auxerre** (Burgundy) is decorated with Romanesque figurative ceiling frescoes dating from the 12th century. The abbey church sits in splendor high above the River Yonne.*

*Below: the entrance to the catacombs of **St. Peter in Salzburg**, which date from late antiquity and are thus the oldest part of the abbey. Chapels were later constructed inside the catacombs—one even sits above the entrance area.*

Opposite: the pre-Romanesque **church of St. Michael in Fulda** *was constructed in 820–22 as the funerary chapel (Germany's oldest) of Fulda Abbey. The central structure is a rotunda above a crypt with eight side columns (symbolizing the Resurrection) and one central pillar.*

The Carolingian imperial abbeys

In conjunction with Pippin the Younger (reigned 741–68), who had dethroned the Merovingians in 754, St. Boniface (672/3–754/5), who came from Wessex and was known as the "Apostle of the Germans," endowed the Frankish Empire with a strict ecclesiastical structure that was loyal to Rome. The next step was to gain control of the large monasteries and force them to adopt the Rule of St. Benedict.

Among the most important monastic centers in the Carolingian lands were the abbeys of St. Gallen, Fulda, and Reichenau. St. Gallen Abbey in Switzerland was founded by St. Othmar in 719, on the spot where the monk and hermit St. Gall had settled in 612. Independent and—before long—wealthy, the abbey resisted until 818 the attempts of the Carolingians to bring it under their control. The powerful abbey survived numerous conflicts with rulers, cities, and the states of the Swiss Confederation and remained a monastic state under the control of a prince-bishop with absolute power and with its own legal jurisdiction until 1798. The abbey was dissolved in 1805.

In 744 St. Boniface instructed his disciple St. Sturmius to found a monastery at Fulda. As the first abbot of Fulda Abbey, Sturmius, who had learned the Rule of St. Benedict at Monte Cassino for this express purpose, succeeded in having the remains of the murdered St. Boniface brought from Mainz to Fulda, making Fulda one of the most important places of pilgrimage north of the Alps.

The St. Gallen monastery plan

Around 830 a monastery plan dedicated to Gozbert of St. Gallen (abbot 816–37) originated in the scriptorium of Reichenau Abbey. Depicting an idealized Benedictine abbey as a self-sufficient, self-contained universe with churches, houses, stables, kitchens, workshops, gardens, breweries, and sick bays, it is the only existing document of its kind dating from before the 13th century. A total of 333 legends explain the functions of the individual buildings.

Whether the plan depicts the conditions that actually prevailed at St. Gallen, or merely represents an ideal ground plan remains the subject of dispute to this day.

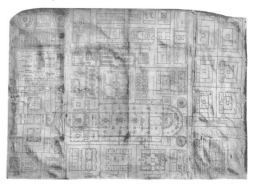

Above: the St. Gallen monastery plan, now in the collection of the library of St. Gallen Abbey, depicts an idealized Benedictine monastery.

Left: the massive complex of **St. Gallen Abbey**, *the church and library of which can be seen here, was rebuilt in the Baroque style after 1755. The ensuing period was to be the abbey's final period of glory.*

*Opposite: the abbey church of St. Salvator—now **Fulda Cathedral**—was built in 1704–12 in Baroque style on the site of the demolished Ratgar Basilica. Like its predecessor, it is based on St. Peter's in Rome.*

*Right: work started on the **Ratgar Basilica**, named after its designer Abbot Ratgar, in 791. It was the largest church of its type north of the Alps and embodied Fulda's ambition to be one of the leading monasteries of its day. The construction of this abbey church, which was demolished in 1700, swallowed up so much money that Abbot Ratgar (abbot 802–17) was finally removed from office by a rebellion of the Fulda monks (illustration based on a model of the Ratgar Basilica).*

*Below: after receiving the relic of St. George, Abbot Hatto III embarked in 900 on the construction of the aisled **abbey church of St. George in Reichenau-Oberzell**, which was subsequently enlarged.*

Until the dawning of the modern age, Fulda was engaged in a constant quarrel with the archbishops of Mainz (one of whom founded Hersfield Abbey in defiance in 769) over its elevated, self-governing status. By the middle of the 9th century, more than 600 monks were already living at Fulda; the Ratgar Basilica, constructed between 791 and 819 in the image of Old St. Peter's in Rome, with two choirs and a west transept, was the largest basilica north of the Alps. In 968 the abbot of Fulda was made primate of all the Benedictine monasteries in Germany. In 1752 Fulda was elevated to the status of princely bishopric before both monastery and principality were dissolved in 1803.

Reichenau Abbey, on the Lake Constance island of the same name, was founded by St. Pirminius in 724 during his campaign to convert the pagan Alemanni. Reichenau became the most famous seat of learning after Fulda, achieving the pinnacle of its power under Hatto III (abbot 888–913), who was also archbishop of Mainz and imperial chancellor. In 896 Hatto received a relic of St. George from the pope and built the abbey church of St. George in which to house it. Reichenau Abbey fell into decline from around 1200 and was eventually dissolved in 1803.

Monasteries as centers of the Carolingian Renaissance

Like the court chapel, the monasteries became seats of learning. Architecturally, Charlemagne's Palatine Chapel in Aachen was not the only building to take its cue from the magnificent edifices of Rome, Constantinople, and Ravenna. Monastic structures were expected not merely to be functional but to impress and (as the St. Gallen monastery plan shows) strove to achieve ideal dimensions and proportions. During this time, the monastic writing schools took on a new lease of life—not least the one at St. Gallen, where the monk Notker Labeo first laid down formal rules for the German language.

As the most important scholar of his day and the author of a 22-volume *Universal Natural History*, Rabanus Maurus (abbot 822–42) developed Fulda Abbey into a major center of learning. Walafrid Strabo, abbot of Reichenau between 839 and 849, whose works include a book on gardening, was probably the most famous writer of his time. Another of Reichenau's author-monks, Hermann the Lame (1013–54), wrote a chronicle of the world and has been credited with the subdivision of the hour into minutes.

*The solid, fortified-looking Carolingian gatehouse of **Frauenchiemsee Abbey** was built in the mid-9th century, probably by Abbess Irmgard, the patron saint of the Chiemgau region. There was a small chapel on the ground floor.*

Other important monasteries in the Frankish Empire

Another important center of book illumination was St. Emmeram's Abbey in Regensburg, built in 739 over the tomb of the missionary and wandering bishop murdered in 652. Initially the abbots of St. Emmeram were also the bishops of Regensburg. The most important of them was the monastery reformer and patron saint of the diocese St. Wolfgang (abbot 972–94). Ever since the 8th century, the Romanesque abbey church with narthex and three choirs has been continually enlarged.

In 782, Duke Tassilo III of Bavaria founded the nunnery of Frauenwörth (Frauenchiemsee) as a counterpart to the monastery of Herrenchiemsee. Frauenwörth came to prominence in 857 when King Louis the German installed his daughter Irmgard there as abbess. The 11th-century abbey church was rebuilt in the Baroque style in the years after 1688. During the 20th century, Romanesque frescoes were uncovered in the choir of the gatehouse and in the abbey church.

The most important monastery for the conversion of northern Germany and Scandinavia was Corvey Abbey in Westphalia, founded in 815 or 822 by Emperor Louis the Pious and monks from Corbie (Corvey: "new Corbie"). One of their number was St. Ansgar (801–65), a missionary in Sweden and the first archbishop of Hamburg and Bremen, who became known as the "Apostle of Scandinavia."

Work started on the construction of the aisled abbey church in 830. The monumental façade flanked by double towers was completed between 873 and 885, which makes it the oldest surviving westwork of any church. It is decorated inside with frescoes depicting scenes from Homer's *Odyssey*. Before long the imperial abbey and diocese possessed one of the world's most important libraries, and it was here in the 10th century that Brother Widukind wrote his history of Saxony. During the Thirty Years War the abbey and with it the library went up in flames. The monastery was subsequently rebuilt in the Baroque style but fell into decline in the 18th century. In 1792 it was made an independent bishopric, but was dissolved just 11 years later.

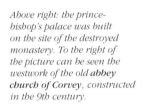

*Above right: the prince-bishop's palace was built on the site of the destroyed monastery. To the right of the picture can be seen the westwork of the old **abbey church** of Corvey, constructed in the 9th century.*

*Right: view of the wall of the narthex, built in 1250, and freestanding bell tower, built in 1575, of **St. Emmeram in Regensburg**. The church was refurbished in the Baroque style by the Brothers Asam between 1731 and 1733.*

The major reform monasteries

During the 10th and 11th centuries, the relaxing of monastic discipline and looming power struggle between emperor and pope led a number of monasteries to initiate reform movements. One important center was Gorze Abbey in Lorraine, founded by Bishop Chrodegang of Metz (c. 715–66). St. Chrodegang was an early ecclesiastical reformer of the Frankish Empire who founded Lorsch Abbey in 764.

In 930, Gorze Abbey became the center of the Gorze Reform, in which it was joined by some 200 monasteries throughout the empire, including St. Gallen, Fulda, Corvey, St. Emmeram in Regensburg, and most importantly Lorsch, which became the leading German abbey of the day. The Gorze Reform argued for stricter monastic discipline but also—as the imperial monasteries were forging close links with their local rulers or the emperor, nurturing their relationships with their worldly benefactors, and educating the administrative elite of the empire in both sacred and secular matters—independence from the pope.

An undeniable self-assurance as a stalwart "fortress of God" is also exhibited by St. Michael's Abbey at Hildesheim, built by Bishop Bernward (in office 993–1022) in 993 and given to the Benedictines in 1010. This politically influential bishop enjoyed a close relationship with the Holy Roman emperors of the Ottonian dynasty (919–1024).

A reform movement diametrically opposed to the Gorze Reform issued from Hirsau Abbey (founded in 765) under Wilhelm, its abbot from 1069 to 1091. Wilhelm imposed on his monks strict discipline, draconian punishments and the highest standards of obedience, and fought for the independence of the monasteries from their secular rulers. He was joined in his reforms, which propagated and adopted the ideas and rules of Cluny, by nearly all the monasteries in southwest Germany. During the Investiture Controversy, which began in 1076, Abbot Wilhelm, as a champion of the freedom of the Church from secular interference, came out emphatically on the side of the pope.

The most important reform monastery was Cluny Abbey, founded by Duke William I of Aquitaine in 910. With the

*Above: Hirsau Abbey was rebuilt in 1059 and the **abbey church of St. Peter and St. Paul** erected between 1083 and 1092. This Romanesque aisled pier basilica with transept was given two west towers in 1120. The abbey was dissolved in 1555.*

*Right: the **abbey church of St. Michael in Hildesheim** is a fine example of Ottonian architecture. The square crossings of this integrally designed building form the basic unit from which the nave and transepts take their structure, with the result that the east and west ends mirror each other perfectly.*

*Opposite page: the gatehouse at **Lorsch Abbey**, known as the "Königshalle," is one of the best preserved of all Carolingian buildings. The ground floor takes the form of an open hall entered through three arches of equal height.*

Right: a famous miniature dating from the time of the Investiture Controversy showing Abbot Hugo of Cluny mediating between his godson, the humbly kneeling Emperor Henry IV, and Countess Matilda of Tuscany, acting on behalf of the pope.

Abbots shape European politics

Cluny soon became known as the "light of the world" and was the center of a sincere movement towards asceticism and piety that attracted pilgrims from all sections of society between the 10th and 12th centuries. The first five abbots were men of strong character who mediated in political conflicts as well as in religious matters.

Cluny experienced its heyday under the administration of St. Odilo (abbot 994–1048), who introduced the festival of All Souls into the Church, and St. Hugo (abbot 1049–1109), who increased the number of Cluny's filiations (daughter monasteries) to 200. Odilo propagated the "peace of God" concept (prohibition of all acts of war in specific places at specific times). Hugo mediated on a number of occasions during the Investiture Controversy (1076–1122) between Pope Gregory VII and Emperor Henry IV, as well as during the emperor's penitential journey to Canossa (1077). The last important abbot of Cluny was the scholar Petrus Venerabilis (abbot 1122–56), who commissioned the first Latin translation of the Qu'ran.

*Right: the surviving parts of the church of the powerful **Cluny Abbey**, whose architecture exerted a decisive influence on the French and German reform monasteries. Only a few monasteries from this period have survived in their original form, however.*

*Below: the chancel of the **abbey church at Cluny** with columns and capitals. One of the chief characteristics of the abbey churches built in the Cluny style was an aisled choir comprising a nave and two side aisles.*

pope's protection, Cluny won the freedom to elect its own abbot without the interference of the secular authorities. The abbey followed a strict version of the Rule of St. Benedict, resisted any attempts to secularize monastic life and, in the liturgical sphere, increased the importance of the Divine Office. Before long, Cluny controlled numerous abbeys and priories (at the peak of its power around 1,200 monasteries and 20,000 brethren). Despite the ascetic lifestyle of the monks, the mighty monastery complex stressed the importance of architectural splendor as a means of glorifying God. The original abbey church (known to architectural historians as Cluny I) was enlarged in 981 (Cluny II) and 1089–95 (Cluny III), eventually taking the form of a nave and four aisles 613 feet (187 meters) in length with two transepts and a vault 100 feet (30.5 meters) in height. Until the construction of St. Peter's in Rome (started in 1506), it was the largest church in Christendom. The abbey was dissolved after 1789 and parts of the complex were blown up in 1810.

Benedictine Abbeys of the Romanesque and Gothic Eras

*Opposite page: the Romanesque central nave of the **abbey church of Vézelay**, which survived the demolition of the monastic buildings in 1796. Between 1185 and 1215 the church was furnished with an Early Gothic choir and transept. Its relics of Mary Magdalene were lost in 1569 during an act of iconoclasm and replaced by new ones in 1870/76.*

*Below left: the **abbey of Mont-Saint-Michel**, which rises majestically and fortress-like above the island, is the focus of numerous legends.*

*Below right: in the 13th century, Philip II Augustus of France sponsored the rebuilding of **St-Michel** in the Gothic style. The resulting architectural ensemble is known as "La Merveille."*

After being plundered by the Normans in 887, Vézelay Abbey, founded in 858/9 by Count Girart II of Vienne, was moved to higher ground and became one of the most important places of pilgrimage in Europe. In 1058 it was subjected to the Cluniac Reform before regaining its independence in 1161.

The main nave of the abbey church of Ste-Marie-Madeleine was constructed between 1120 and 1140. The abbey had held relics of Mary Magdalene since the 9th century and developed into the center of the cult of the saint in Europe (numerous accounts exist of miraculous healing) for pilgrims following the Way of St. James to Santiago de Compostela. It was here in 1146 that St. Bernard of Clairvaux preached the Second Crusade.

The narthex was built between 1140 and 1152 and has a tympanum (decorative panel) above the main door depicting the enthroned Christ as judge. The church was to become famous throughout the world, however, for its 99 column capitals in the nave depicting lively scenes from the Old and New Testaments and moralizing representations of good and evil. These capitals were designed as a visual representation of the Christian message for the enlightenment of the pilgrims. In 965/6, Benedictine monks founded the Abbey of Mont-Saint-Michel on the island where, in 708, according to legend, Archangel Michael had commanded the bishop of Avranches to build a church. Between 1017 and 1520, a fortress-like complex of monastery buildings gradually developed. The first, Romanesque-style, abbey church was erected between 1023 and 1084 before being rebuilt in the Gothic style in the 13th century.

Richly endowed by the French kings and the dukes of Normandy, the abbey became an important place of pilgrimage in the 12th century and one of Normandy's major intellectual centers. During the Hundred Years War (1337–1453), however, it was partly destroyed by the English. In 1469 it became the seat of its own order of knights, the Order of Saint-Michel. The abbey was dissolved in 1790, although in 1969 a small Benedictine community once again took up residence on the island. Numerous legends have sprung up around the abbey, most of them concerning the Holy Grail.

Monasteries in Italy

The nunnery complex of San Salvatore and Santa Giulia in Brescia was built over Roman ruins by the last Lombard king, Desiderius, and his wife Ansa. It was intended as a royal burial place and endowed with relics of the martyred St. Julia. Subsequent Carolingian rulers were also generous towards the convent and used it as a political power base in northern Italy: several princesses in the line of King Lothair I occupied the position of abbess here between 851 and 896.

In 762/3 the basilica of San Salvatore was given a crypt that was subsequently extended in the 12th century. In or around 1300 it received a campanile (bell tower), whose lower portion was decorated with frescoes, and later in the 14th century a side chapel was added. In 1466 the façade was demolished and a nun's choir built as an entrance lobby. This now forms part of the convent chapel of Santa Giulia. The two stories of this choir were decorated with magnificent frescoes depicting the life of Jesus in the form of a processional route from birth to the Passion.

In the 12th century, the convent acquired another place of worship, the church of Santa Maria in Solario, which served as its memorial chapel. This square space is crowned by an octagonal cupola. The ground floor houses numerous relics and convent treasures including a fine example of 8th-century goldwork: the cross of the Lombard king Desiderius (from Brescia), who was dethroned by Charlemagne in 774. The upper story was used for liturgical purposes. It has a groin vault decorated with stars, while its walls are adorned with 16th-century frescoes.

The convent became involved in the 12th century in the dispute between the self-assured Lombard League and the emperor—a conflict in which Brescia played a leading role. In 1512 both city and convent were plundered by the French, and after 1600 the majority of Brescia's churches—including parts of the convent complex—were rebuilt in the Baroque style. The convent was dissolved in 1798 and served as a military depot until 1882, when it was restored and turned into a museum which houses valuable artefacts related to the convent and the Lombardy region.

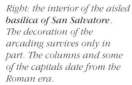

*Opposite page above: the **crypt of San Salvatore**, intended as the burial chamber of the Lombard kings. The capitals of a number of its antique columns are decorated with plant motifs.*

*Left: the first courtyard of the **convent complex in Brescia**. The large building with bell tower (campanile) on the right is the large convent church of Santa Giulia. To its left is the basilica (with side aisles) of San Salvatore. The abbey was one of the most important in northern Italy.*

*Right: the interior of the aisled **basilica of San Salvatore**. The decoration of the arcading survives only in part. The columns and some of the capitals date from the Roman era.*

Monasteries in Germany

The church known today as the Kaisersdom (Imperial Cathedral) in Königslutter was originally part of the Benedictine abbey of St. Peter and St. Paul, founded by Emperor Lothair III of Supplinburg in 1135. When the emperor died in 1137, he was buried in the unfinished abbey church, which was only completed under Duke Henry the Lion in 1170.

The monk's choir forming the east end of the church was built between 1135 and 1150 in the Cluny style. The rather plain and ascetic west end and nave were completed between 1150 and 1160. The two west towers were only added in the 15th century.

Königslutter was modeled on northern Italian cathedral architecture. The influence can be seen in the lion door of the north transept. The door is flanked by two lions supporting twisted columns on their backs. Work on a cloister with ornamental columns and capitals began in 1150. The abbey was presented with relics by Lothair and his successors and became an important place of pilgrimage in northern Germany. It was dissolved under the Reformation in 1570.

The only well-preserved Holy Sepulcher dating from the Romanesque period is located at the Schottenkloster in Eichstätt, an abbey with a hospital (lepers' house) attached to it, which is thought to have been founded by Irish monks in 1148. In 1166 Walbrun of Rieshofen, the dean of Eichstätt Cathedral, ordained the construction of a copy of the tomb of Christ in Jerusalem (in the form it took in the mid-12th century) and entrusted the project to the abbey's monks. It is believed that Walbrun had taken part in the Second Crusade of 1147 and visited Christ's tomb while in the Holy Land. An oval mortuary chapel, the Church of the Holy Cross, decorated with a round-arch frieze, was erected around the Holy Sepulcher and consecrated in 1194. A square vestibule with three entrances was built on the south side. The Schottenkloster was dissolved in 1493, having stood empty since 1460. Responsibility for maintaining the monument, which had fallen into disrepair, passed to the Capuchin monks who had been summoned to Eichstätt in 1623. Today the Holy Sepulcher is located in the east side chapel of the Capuchin church built in 1623–26.

Right: the present-day **Kaisersdom in Königslutter** *was originally a Romanesque abbey church reminiscent of northern Italian ecclesiastical architecture. Towards the end of the 19th century (1887–94), the church interior was painted in a style based on medieval church decoration.*

Opposite page: the only well-preserved example of a Holy Sepulcher from the Romanesque era is the tall monument (13½ feet/ 4.1 meters) located above a dark burial chamber in the **Chapel of the Holy Sepulcher of the Schottenkloster** *in Eichstätt. The antechamber contains a stone cube known as the "Angel Stone."*

*Right: the gatehouse of **Maria Laach Abbey**. Parts of the abbey complex were destroyed in a fire in 1855 and subsequently rebuilt.*

*Opposite page above: between 1220 and 1230 a chapel dedicated to St. Nicholas was built onto **Maria Laach Abbey**. It incorporated a "paradise" in the form of a colonnaded atrium.*

*Below: general view of **Maria Laach Abbey** on the shores of Lake Laach. Maria Laach is one of Germany's best-appointed abbeys, with its own farm, organic produce outlets, tourist facilities, lakeside hotel, publishing house, and workshops.*

The Benedictine abbey of Maria Laach in Germany's Eifel region was founded in 1093 by Count Henry II of Laach and his wife Adelheid. Dedicated to the Virgin Mary and St. Nicholas, it became a self-governing abbey in 1138. Although the abbey church was not completed until 1156, the foundations for its crypt, nave, crossing tower, westwork, and east end had been laid by the end of 1093. To prevent periodic flooding, the monks dug a canal to divert the lake's floodwaters. Between 1230 and 1250, Gothic-style modifications to the nave were undertaken, involving the installation of stone vaulting to replace the flat wooden ceiling.

This complex shares many features with the St. Gallen monastery plan, but also with the imperial cathedrals of Speyer, Mainz, and Worms. The abbey was at the height of its glory as a center of learning between 1300 and 1450. Having been partially rebuilt in the Baroque style during the 17th and 18th centuries, the abbey was dissolved in 1802 before eventually devolving to the Jesuit order in 1863. Since 1892 it has been occupied once more by the Benedictine order.

The monastery garden

The monastery garden served primarily as a kitchen garden and contributed to the self-sufficiency of the monastery by providing the monks with fruit, vegetables, and herbs. The Benedictine and Cistercian orders felt a particular obligation to cultivate and exploit nature. "Decorative and recreational" gardens came later, and were often combined with the herb garden. Monks' knowledge of plants and their properties developed into considerable medical expertise that often incorporated popular cures as well. In this field the Benedictine nun Hildegard of Bingen (1098–1179) was pioneering.

The emphasis placed on the religious symbolism of the garden, either as a "paradise garden" (an earthly reflection of paradise), or as a place for the veneration of the Virgin Mary (based on the symbol of the rose without a thorn), grew stronger over time. Monasteries also conducted practical experiments with plants, aimed, for example, at improving the quality of wine and fruit. Through his experimental crossing of purebred pea plants, the "father of genetics" Gregor Mendel (1822–84), abbot of the Augustinian abbey of Alt-Brünn, ultimately came up with his Laws of Inheritance.

*Many monasteries—including **Maria Laach**, shown above—use their monastery gardens as nurseries. The income from the sale of plants contributes to the upkeep of the monastery.*

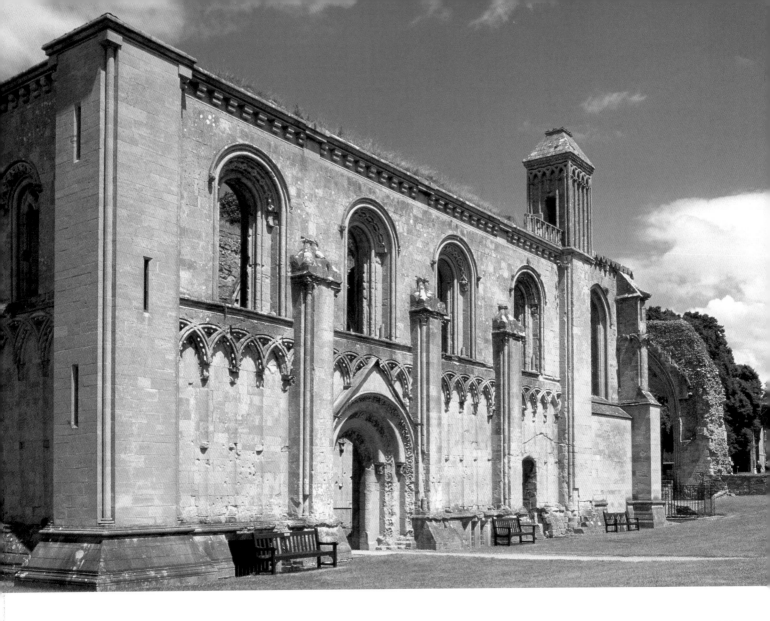

Above: the ruins of **Glastonbury Abbey**. *The monument to King Arthur and his consort, erected in 1278, was destroyed sometime after 1534. In 1962 two skeletons were discovered but their identities remain under dispute.*

Right: the full and impressive extent of **Glastonbury Abbey**, *one of Great Britain's most important early monasteries (drawing based on a wooden model).*

*Left: one of the few surviving portions of **Bury St. Edmunds Abbey**, which nevertheless conveys a good impression of the sturdy construction of this large fortified abbey built in the 11th century.*

*Left: in 1214 **Bury St. Edmunds Abbey**, of which only the ruins survive today, was the meeting place of the lords and bishops who drew up the Magna Carta. With this document, signed the following year, they forced the king to grant certain inalienable rights.*

Monasteries in England

Numerous legends have grown up around Glastonbury Abbey, which is now thought to have been founded in the 6th century. Believed at one time to have been founded (by disciples of Jesus) even earlier, it was later associated with Joseph of Arimathea, who is supposed to have brought the Holy Grail here after Christ's crucifixion.

Abbot Dunstan (in office 945–57), a future archbishop of Canterbury, introduced the Rule of St. Benedict. In 1191 the large abbey attained even greater importance when, following a serious fire in 1184, monks discovered a tombstone complete with inscription and lead cross, beneath which lay a male and a female skeleton. On the basis of the inscription the remains were identified as those of King Arthur and Queen Guinevere. This made the abbey a place of pilgrimage and so it remains—for lovers of mysteries—to this day. At the time of its dissolution by the Crown in 1534, only 51 brethren were living at the abbey. The last abbot, Richard Whyting, was executed in 1539 for resisting the dissolution of his abbey.

Another important English monastery was Bury St. Edmunds, founded by King Sigebert of East Anglia in 633. The abbey acquired its name when the mortal remains of St. Edmund, king of East Anglia (reigned 855–69) were brought here in 903. Edmund had been killed in 869 while resisting the pagan Danes (Vikings) and was considered to be a Christian martyr.

Tales of numerous miraculous cures at his tomb led to rich endowments from the English kings. It became one of England's biggest monasteries and, after 1020, was rebuilt on a cruciform ground plan and the abbey church of St. James constructed. The remains and relics of St. Edmund were translated to the new church in 1095.

In 1327 the abbey, which had been granted overlordship of the town of the same name in 942/5, fell victim to a revolt against its monastic privileges by the local people. Over the next two centuries it was completely rebuilt (with the famous mid-14th-century Abbeygate). The work was completed by 1506, but in 1539 the abbey was dissolved. Today most of its buildings lie in ruins.

Famous abbey churches

One of the most famous abbey churches of the Gothic period is Westminster Abbey. While tradition has it that the abbey was founded in 616, it is thought more likely that it dates from around 750. The monastery was given to the Benedictines by St. Dunstan, archbishop of Canterbury 960–78. King Edward the Confessor built the monastery church between 1045 and 1065 and his remains were interred here in 1163 following his canonization.

Starting with William the Conqueror (1066), Westminster was adopted as the traditional place of coronation of the English and subsequently British sovereigns; it is also the burial place of 17 of the nation's monarchs. Westminster Abbey acquired its current Gothic aspect between 1245 and 1517. Its numerous chapels contain the remains of many famous British citizens. One such chapel is the memorial chapel of Edward the Confessor, which for centuries contained the coronation throne (King Edward's Chair). Another chapel of particular note is the Late Gothic chapel (built between 1503 and 1519) of Henry VII, remarkable for its ceiling. The monastery was dissolved in 1539 and the cathedral brought under the control of the Crown as the collegiate church of St. Peter.

Equally famous is the cathedral of the abbey of Saint-Denis in Paris, which is the burial place of numerous Merovingian and Carolingian rulers and nearly all the French kings since Hugo Capet (reigned 987–96).

The current church is based on plans drawn up by the famous Abbot Suger (in office 1122–51), a onetime regent of France who began work on the west end in 1130. The west front was completed in 1137 and features a dramatic doorway with a tympanum depicting Christ as Judge of the World. The most important architectural element is the choir with ambulatory and radiating chapels, begun in 1136. For the first time ever, ambulatory and chapels were spanned by a single rib vault, creating a unified space and earning Saint-Denis a reputation as one of the birthplaces of Gothic architecture. The new method of construction made possible large, high windows that flooded the entire church with light. The overall design accorded with Abbot Suger's doctrine of harmony, whereby the architecture was to serve two purposes at the same time: the glorification of God and the edification of the faithful.

*Opposite page: built between 1722 and 1745, the towers were a later addition to the 15th-century west front of **Westminster Abbey in London**. Statesmen and poets are buried in the abbey in addition to members of the royal family.*

*Below left: the façade of the north transept of **Westminster Abbey** with its Gothic flying buttresses; behind is the chapel of Edward the Confessor.*

*Below right: the Early Gothic ambulatory of **Saint-Denis**, to the north of Paris. The church is also famous for its "pierced triforium," a wall passage looking onto the nave which is flooded with light from windows in its outer wall. This was built between 1231 and 1281.*

Early Cistercian Abbeys

Cîteaux, the mother abbey of the Cistercian order, was founded in 1098 in a swampy region of Burgundy to which St. Robert of Molesme (c. 1028–1111) had withdrawn. Together with a small number of companions, Robert wanted to revive the original monastic ideals of St. Benedict of Nursia. The community initially labored hard to cultivate the land, something all the early Cistercian foundations had in common.

The real organizer of the abbey and order, however, was Robert's successor, Englishman Stephen Harding (abbot 1109–34), who drew up the order's rule (the *Charta caritatis*) and completed a translation of the Bible that was binding for all Cistercian abbeys. It was he who created the order's strict hierarchical system of mother and daughter abbeys.

The original buildings of Cîteaux Abbey no longer survive. The earliest surviving structures are the library of 1498–1509 and the administrative building on which work began in 1636. A new abbey church with cloister was completed by 1772. Dissolved in 1797, the abbey has been occupied by Trappist monks since 1898.

The mother abbeys in France

The years after 1113 saw the founding of the first four filiations of the Cistercian order. La Ferté, Pontigny, and Morimond were followed in 1115 by Clairvaux, which was established by the outstanding preacher and devoted servant of the order St. Bernard of Clairvaux (1090–1153), with whose name the rise of the Cistercians is inextricably linked.

During Bernard's lifetime, Clairvaux in turn established no fewer than 166 daughter and "granddaughter" abbeys, all of which bore the theological and architectural stamp of Clairvaux. One of the common architectural features was a Romanesque rib vault of unique design, based on ribs with a square profile (box ribs). All the building work was carried out by lay brothers (also known as *conversi*) of the abbeys.

The original monastery buildings at Clairvaux were completed by 1135, but were continually expanded in the years up to 1708. Between 1148 and 1174, for example, an abbey church 394 feet (120 meters) long with ambulatory and radiating chapels was erected. In 1792 the abbey was dissolved and partly demolished. The surviving buildings have been used as a prison since 1808.

*Right: the surviving buildings of the celebrated **Clairvaux Abbey**, whose abbot St. Bernard has dominated the public image of the order right up to the present day. The property passed into the ownership of the French state in 1792 and has been used as a penal institution for more than 200 years.*

*Left: **Cîteaux**, the Cistercian mother abbey. The order's early abbeys are distinguished by their architectural simplicity and lack of decoration.*

*Opposite page: a Trappist monk in front of **Cîteaux Abbey**. The Trappists are a strict reform branch of the Cistercian order that seeks to revive the order's original ascetic orientation.*

Fontenay Abbey was founded by St. Bernard in 1119 as a daughter abbey of Clairvaux. The chosen site was a wilderness that first had to be cleared. Fish ponds were established to feed the monks, 200 of whom lived here during the heyday of the abbey. Fontenay is the best preserved of all the early Cistercian abbeys and many parts survive in their original condition. With its simple, unadorned façades and lack of church tower, the complex follows the austere ideals of the order in its early days.

Construction of the abbey church began in 1139. The eight-bay nave is 217 feet (66 meters) long and lit by the windows of the two side aisles alone, although light also enters the church from the east wall behind the altar (sanctuary) and west wall. The roof takes the form of a pointed barrel vault with broad transverse arches. The church possesses a Gothic altar and a 13th-century stone Madonna, the "Madonna of Fontenay." The church was consecrated in 1147 by the first Cistercian pope, Eugene III (reigned 1145–53), a disciple of St. Bernard who had come to Clairvaux as a monk in 1138.

Adjoining the south transept is a low-ceilinged chapter house, the monks' place of assembly, which dates from 1150 and displays various Gothic stylistic elements. Above this is the large dormitory in which the monks slept side by side on thin straw mattresses, separated one from another by nothing more than low wooden partitions.

The cloister, with its double arcades and double columns, is regarded as a masterpiece of Romanesque architecture. In line with the ideal Cistercian ground plan, Fontenay, like all the order's other early abbeys, was constructed as a double monastery in which the monks' domain was distinct from that of the lay brothers (*conversi*). The main responsibility of the latter was to run the abbey farms with their extensive fields and forests. Later buildings at Fontenay include the abbot's palace, which was built in the 18th century in Rococo style.

In 1791 the abbey was dissolved and used as a paper mill. A program of careful restoration was embarked upon in 1906, which succeeded in preserving the complex of buildings for posterity.

*A view of the courtyard of the Romanesque cloister at **Fontenay Abbey**. The double columns, compact buttresses, and pointed barrel vault create an impression of strength and stockiness.*

*Opposite page above: the interior of the monks' simple dormitory at **Fontenay**. The lay brothers had their own separate wing and dormitory.*

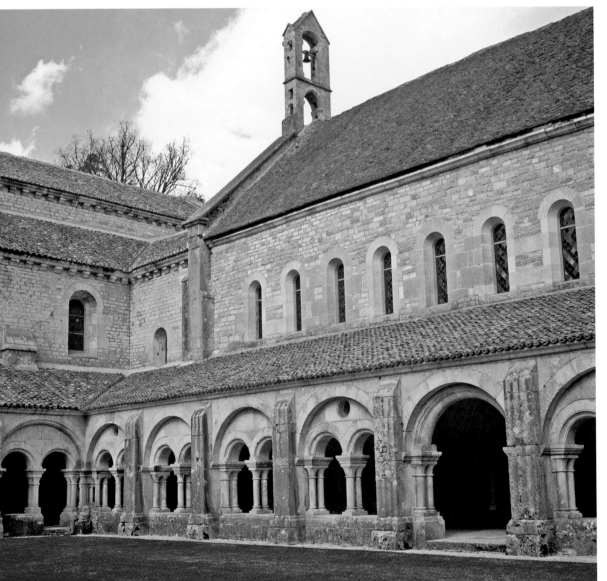

*Opposite page below: the monks' dormitory at **Fontenay** from the outside. Next door to the dormitory is the infirmary. The abbey church can be seen in the background.*

*Interior view of the cloister at **Fontfroide Abbey**, one of the best known and most beautiful cloisters of the Middle Ages. In 1250, work began on the construction of a Gothic-style ceiling vault and upper story.*

The abbey of Sainte-Marie de Fontfroide was founded in 1093. Initially a Benedictine house, it moved to the Cistercians in 1146 following a visit by St. Bernard of Clairvaux. Work started the same year on the abbey church with pointed barrel vault which, despite its simplicity, is impressive for its size. Also dating from the Late Romanesque period are the cloister and chapter house, built between 1180 and 1210. Around 1250 the entire cloister complex was rebuilt in the Gothic style and a large tracery (decorative filigree stonework) window added. Further extensive building work was undertaken during the fifteenth century, including the construction of Gothic side chapels on the south side.

The abbey played a leading role in the battle against the Cathars in southern France. The assassination in 1208 of papal legate Pierre de Castelnau, a monk from Fontfroide, provoked a series of bloody crusades against the Cathars. Jacques Fournier, abbot of Fontfroide between 1311 and 1317, later became Pope Benedict XII (reigned 1334–42). Dissolved in 1791 and reoccupied by monks between 1858 and 1901, the abbey was acquired at auction by a pair of art lovers in 1908 and carefully restored.

The pharmacy of the **Dominican monastery of San Marco in Florence**, rebuilt between 1437 and 1452, demonstrates the importance attached by monasteries throughout history to the production of medicines and tinctures.

Monasteries and the care of the sick

Care of the sick is one of the seven acts of compassion described by Christ during his final days (Matthew 25, 34–46). The performance of these acts, which are also described in Christ's parable of the Good Samaritan (Luke 10, 25–37), is necessary in order to find mercy in the eyes of God.

Even the early abbeys had infirmaries. These were not just for the benefit of members of the monastic community. Especially those abbeys positioned along pilgrim routes took care of lay people and pilgrims in need. Many monasteries had medicinal herb gardens; the monks were familiar with the curative properties of certain plants and used them to relieve not only physical pain but mental anguish as well.

Later, individual orders—such as that of St. John of Jerusalem or the women's orders dedicated to the ideals of Elizabeth of Hungary (1207–31), who established a hospital in Marburg—dedicated themselves specifically to the care of the sick and also performed such work in mission lands.

*Right: the monks' dormitory at **Fontfroide**, which is simple and solid-looking in the style of the early Cistercian abbeys. The dormitory of the lay brothers was converted into a guest wing in the 15th century.*

Cistercian abbeys in Italy

Fossanova was founded as a Benedictine abbey by the count of Aquino some time before 800. St. Thomas Aquinas (1225–74), the founder's most famous scion and the preeminent thinker of the Middle Ages, died in the abbey's pilgrims' lodgings in March 1274. The abbey had adopted the Cistercian Rule in 1135 during Bernard of Clairvaux's journey to Italy.

Construction of the Late Romanesque and Early Gothic abbey complex with cloister began in 1173. Work began on the abbey church, central Italy's earliest Gothic edifice, in 1187. It is modeled on the architectural rules drawn up by St. Bernard, with two transept chapels. The nave is spanned by a groin vault with transverse arches. The church, whose emphatic simplicity extends to its façade and main door, was consecrated by Pope Innocent II (reigned 1198–1216) in 1208. Further buildings in the Gothic style, such as the refectory (dining hall) and chapter house, were added to the complex between 1280 and 1310. The abbey was dissolved in 1810 but was given to the Carthusian order in 1825 and subsequently the Polish Franciscans in 1932.

In 1141 Duke Garnerio of Spoleto founded the abbey of Santa Maria di Chiaravalle di Fiastra, and Cistercian monks from Chiaravalle Milanese moved in the following year. Here too the cruciform abbey church, built of brick, follows the ground plan established by St. Bernard, with a nave and two side aisles, a square choir (chancel), and a transept with two barrel-vaulted side chapels. The westernmost of the nave's four bays has a simple groin vault. Adjoining the west end is a porch, and a marble rose window was later added to the façade above. The only remaining part of the original monastery buildings is the six-bay chapter house in the east wing. All the other parts have been subsequently rebuilt.

After suffering war damage in the years after 1422, the monastery fell into decline and was given to the Jesuit order in 1581. It was eventually dissolved in 1773 and became the country seat of the local lord. Since 1985 a small Cistercian community has again been living at Chiaravalle di Fiastra.

Opposite page above: the simple Romanesque colonnaded cloister on the Cistercian model at the **abbey of Santa Maria di Chiaravalle di Fiastra.**

Opposite page below: in 1135, **Fossanova Abbey** *placed itself under the charge of the Cistercian abbey of Hautecome in Savoy, a filiation of Clairvaux, and in turn became the mother abbey of five further Cistercian houses.*

Above: the **abbey of Santa Maria di Chiaravalle di Fiastra** *developed into one of the most important monasteries in the Italian Marches.*

Right: the simple, solid-looking method of construction of the early Cistercian monasteries is in evidence here in the refectory (dining hall) at **Chiaravalle di Fiastra.**

Cistercian monasteries in Germany

The Cistercians were made particularly welcome in the economically less well-developed east of Germany. They began by draining the land—their abbeys were nearly always located in marshy regions; they then received or bought from the ruler villages and lakes that they managed. Zinna Abbey, for example, possessed 116 square miles (300 square kilometers) of manorial lands at its peak in 1307.

The monks were used as instruments of colonization, responsible for Christianizing the first Slavs—albeit with some resistance: in 1179 Rizzo, Zinna's first abbot, and in 1185 Sibold, the first abbot of Lehnin, were killed by local Slavs.

Zinna Abbey was founded by Archbishop Wichmann of Magdeburg in 1170. After its destruction by the Slavs in 1179, it was rebuilt from 1221 onwards. The abbey church, completed in 1226, is an Early Gothic pier basilica of field stone. In 1350 the complex was expanded through the addition of the "New Abbey," with guesthouse and infirmary. The abbey was dissolved in 1553 and restored from 1897 onwards. Lehnin Abbey was founded by the margrave of Brandenburg of the Ascanian dynasty in 1180 as a daughter house of Morimond Abbey. In 1258 Chorin Abbey was in turn established by Lehnin. Both are typical examples of the German Brick Gothic style. At Lehnin the monks baked the bricks themselves in enormous ovens—up to 10,000 units at a time.

Work started on the eastern portion of the abbey church at Lehnin (crossing, chancel, and transepts) in 1185. The rib vault was completed by around 1220 and the cloister by 1235. Before long, Lehnin accommodated a community of 100 brethren, and from as early as 1250 the complex was extended several times and the west front completed.

The abbey church with nave and two side aisles at Chorin is modeled on the church at Lehnin but also incorporates various architectural elements that are typical of the mendicant orders. The west front with its lancet windows and famous gable is more showy and highly decorated than other abbey churches in the Brick Gothic style.

The abbey buildings, rib vaults, and cloisters of Chorin survive in a semi-ruined state. Both monasteries were dissolved in 1542 during the Reformation and subsequently fell into decay. A program of careful restoration work was embarked upon in the 19th century.

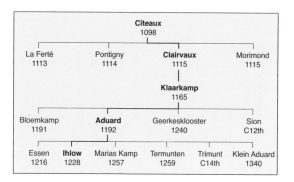

			Cîteaux 1098		
La Ferté 1113		Pontigny 1114		**Clairvaux** 1115	Morimond 1115
			Klaarkamp 1165		
Bloemkamp 1191		**Aduard** 1192	Geerkesklooster 1240		Sion C12th
Essen 1216	**Ihlow** 1228	Marias Kamp 1257	Termunten 1259	Trimunt C14th	Klein Aduard 1340

Left: line of filiation of the Cistercian abbey of Ihlow in East Frisia. During times of difficulty and uncertainty, daughter abbeys would turn to their mother abbey for help. The abbots of the mother abbeys made regular visits (visitatio) to their daughter monasteries in order to keep a check on them and receive their reports.

*Opposite page: the sober interior of the **abbey church of St. Maria at Lehnin** looking east. Simple decorative friezes and use of the grisaille technique (the painting of monochrome plant motifs on the windows) emphasize the plainness of the design.*

*Below left: the brewhouse, lay brother wing, and in the background the **abbey church at Chorin**. The austerity of the façades is offset to a certain extent by the stepped gables with their decorative pinnacles.*

*Below right: the infirmary and other abbey buildings at **Zinna Abbey** in the Uckermark region of Germany. Late Gothic vaulting was introduced in the side aisles and transepts during subsequent rebuilding.*

*Opposite page: **Dunbrody Abbey** is Ireland's best-preserved 12th-century monastery ruin. The nave arcading and large west front window collapsed in 1852.*

*Left: the surviving parts of **Fountains Abbey**, most importantly the church walls and tower, have been carefully maintained since 1852.*

Cistercian abbeys in Great Britain and Ireland

*Below: the surviving walls and arcading of the **abbey church at Rievaulx**. The monastery was the center of the cult of St. Aelred, one of its abbots.*

The unforgiving environs of North Yorkshire in the north of England were another region the Cistercians succeeded in rendering fertile. In 1132 Thurstan, archbishop of York between 1114 and 1190, founded the abbeys of Rievaulx and Fountains, which grew powerful through sheep breeding and dairy and fish-farming.

Within ten years there were 300 monks living at Rievaulx. By the end of St. Aelred's incumbency (1147–67), the renowned abbot had increased their number to over 650 monks and lay brothers. Between 1215 and 1220 the abbey church, originally constructed 1135–45 with a nave and two side aisles and double arcading, was given a new choir with five altars, bringing its total length to 341 feet (104 meters). In addition to the walls of the church, the surviving parts of the abbey include the walls of the aisled chapter house, the refectory, and an infirmary wing with its own cloister and a sick ward. Like Fountains, Rievaulx met its downfall in the 14th century through a combination of the "Black Death" (the plague) and the border wars with Scotland. By 1381 only 14 monks remained at the abbey and in 1538 it was dissolved.

At Fountains Abbey, reconstruction work began in 1147 following the destruction of the original buildings. The single-nave church was expanded between 1155 and 1160 and provided with two barrel-vaulted side aisles. Of the monastery buildings, the church walls and the remains of the chapter house, refectory, workshops, and lay brothers' wing still stand. The abbey was dissolved in 1539.

Following the conquest of Ireland by the Normans, Dunbrody Abbey was founded in 1170 by the Norman nobleman Hervé de Montmorency, who also served as its first abbot (between 1170 and 1205). The cruciform abbey church with chapels on the eastern side of its transepts was built between 1210 and 1240, and a crossing tower added in the 15th century. All that now remains of the monastery buildings are the eastern tower and a door arch in the west. The abbey was dissolved and plundered in 1536 and was transferred to the English Crown in 1542.

The Monasteries
of the New Orders

In the 11th century, numerous new orders started to emerge that built impressive monastery complexes. The architectural form of these buildings was often determined by the orientation of the order in question.

The monasteries of the Premonstratensians and Dominicans

The Premonstratensian order was strongly influenced by the ideas of the Cistercians, but has always combined monastic life with the pastoral care of a local parish. Teplá Monastery in the Czech Republic was founded in 1193 by Count Hroznata, a Bohemian nobleman who entered the abbey himself as a monk in 1202. The collegiate church of the Annunciation, a hall church built in a transitional Romanesque–Gothic style, was consecrated in 1232.

*The austere interior of the **abbey church of San Nicolò in Treviso**. Part of the church was damaged when the tower collapsed in the fourteenth century; the tower was subsequently rebuilt.*

Located at the center of an area that was beginning to be settled by German colonists, the fortunes of the richly appointed monastery improved significantly after 1380. During the Thirty Years War (1618–48), it was plundered on two occasions and was completely destroyed by fire in 1659. A new church and abbey were erected in the Baroque style under Raimund Wilfert II (abbot 1688–1722). The church was decorated with frescoes and was given a magnificent new high altar in 1750. During this time the Teplá monks played a leading role in the academic life of Bohemia. In 1818 Karl Reitenberger (abbot 1813–27) founded the famous spa town of Marienbad. After World War II, the monks were turned out and the monastery was dissolved a few years later. Premonstratensian monks eventually returned to Teplá Monastery in 1990.

The Dominican friar-preachers, another mendicant order, also performed active pastoral work. Work started on

Above: the **collegiate church of the Premonstratensian monastery at Teplá**, with adjoining monastic buildings, was reworked by the Bavarian Baroque architect Christoph Dientzenhofer (1655–1722) after 1689.

the construction of the Dominican monastery and church of San Nicolò in Treviso (Italy), an Early Gothic brick church with round piers and a cloister, in 1282. Following a number of structural changes, it was not completed until 1389. The famous chapter-house frescoes were made possible by legacies from Pope Benedict XI (reigned 1303–04). The free exchange of opinions has always played an important role among the Dominicans, and the chapter house is where discussions and votes were held.

The walls of the chapter house are decorated with 40 frescoes depicting famous members of the order—including popes, cardinals, and important thinkers such as Albertus Magnus and Thomas Aquinas. These portraits, by the painter Tomaso da Modena (c. 1325–79), also include the earliest-known depiction of a pair of spectacles. The roof and tower of the church, as well as some of the chapter-house frescoes were badly damaged by aerial bombs in 1944, but they were later restored.

Left: a Dominican friar at study, from the famous cycle of frescoes in the chapter house at San Nicolò in Treviso, painted by Tomaso da Modena (1352 onwards).

Assisi and the Franciscans

The monastery buildings at Assisi are inextricably linked with the Franciscan order. The foundation stone of the church of San Francesco was laid by the pope in 1228, the year of Francis of Assisi's canonization. Work on the Sacro Convento (Holy Convent), the mother monastery of the Franciscans, started the same year.

The basilica, which incorporates both Romanesque and Gothic stylistic elements, takes the form of a double church. The Lower Church (Basilica Inferiore), to where the remains of St. Francis were translated in 1230, was completed in 1239. Its nave is decorated with the oldest frescoes depicting the life of the order's founder, which survive only in part. The Upper Church (Basilica Superiore), completed in 1259, is one of the most famous of all Christian churches, mainly because of the cycle of frescoes by Giotto di Bondone (1266–1337) depicting 14 lively scenes from the life of St. Francis which portray the saint, with apocalyptic overtones, as a true imitator of Christ. Also famous is the rose window above the entrance to the upper church (see p. 2).

*Opposite page: the interior of the **Upper Church of San Francesco at Assisi**, looking east. Giotto's frescoes can be seen on the walls.*

*Right: the choir stalls (wooden with inlaid work) in the **Upper Church of San Francesco at Assisi**.*

*Below: the **Upper Church of San Francesco at Assisi** showing the bell tower, which was completed in 1239. The complex has repeatedly suffered severe damage as a result of earthquakes, most recently in 1997.*

St. Francis of Assisi: the radical imitation of Christ

St. Francis preaching to Pope Honorius III (reigned 1216–27), who finally approved the order's rule in 1223 (painting from Giotto's cycle of frescoes).

Francis of Assisi (1181/2–1226) is a provocative exception even among Christian saints. Having grown up as the son of a prosperous cloth merchant, this soldier and man of the world was taken prisoner during battle and underwent a radical transformation during the years 1204/05. He gave away his possessions and renounced all worldly belongings, living initially as a hermit and rebuilding dilapidated chapels with his own hands, among them the famous Portiuncula near Assisi, where he lived from 1208. His small band of followers grew rapidly and the pope provisionally confirmed his rule in 1210 while repeatedly requiring him to tone it down. The first Franciscan monastery was founded in 1212. In addition to unconditional submission to "Lady Poverty" in imitation of Christ, through his prayers and chants St. Francis propagated a pious love of nature and charitable love of one's neighbor. After withdrawing into solitude in 1224, St. Francis received the stigmata of Christ on his body, the first known case of stigmatization.

*Interior of the **church of Santa Maria in Aracoeli in Rome**, showing its arcading, fashioned from antique columns, and magnificent ceiling.*

Among the other important Franciscan churches and monasteries at Assisi is the convent and church complex of San Damiano, located below the town. San Damiano was a dilapidated chapel rebuilt by St. Francis from 1205 onward as a simple place of prayer exhibiting a closeness to nature. This is also where, in 1224/5, he composed what is perhaps his most famous prayer, the *Canticle of the Sun*. The main nave of the church, which is connected via a cloister to the convent, contains 14th-century frescoes depicting scenes from the life of the saint.

San Damiano is also the place where St. Clare of Assisi (1193/4–1253), a companion of St. Francis and founder of a female branch of the Franciscan order, the Poor Clares, died. To her is dedicated the Gothic church of Santa Chiara in Assisi, with its red and white striped façade, on which work started in 1257. In the sanctuary of this church hangs the wooden cross of San Damiano from which Christ was supposed to have spoken to St. Francis.

During the 13th and 14th centuries, this church and its side chapels were decorated with numerous important cycles of frescoes by artists whose names are no longer known. Another important Franciscan church is that of Santa Maria in Aracoeli in Rome. The structure that preceded it—where St. Helena, the mother of Emperor Constantine was buried—had been erected on the site of a Roman temple to Juno that contained the "heavenly altar" (Latin: *ara coeli*) from which the later church takes its name.

In 1250 the pope gave the monastery complex occupying the site, which had housed Greek monks since the 8th century, to the Franciscans. They in turn erected a monastery church with a nave and two side aisles whose arcading incorporates 22 columns salvaged from antique buildings. The magnificent coffered ceiling was donated by Pope Gregory XIII in memory of the Battle of Lepanto (1571) in which the Christian fleet defeated the Ottoman Turks. The church is famous for its figure of the Christ Child, believed to work miracles, which was carved by a Franciscan father out of olivewood from the Garden of Gethsemane. A flight of 124 steep steps leading up to the outwardly rather plain church was completed in 1348.

Right: general view of the **church and convent of Santa Chiara at Assisi**. *After the discovery of the remains of St. Clare here in 1850, a new crypt was built to house them and was finished by 1872.*

Below: frescoes in the **chapel of San Damiano near Assisi**. *The painting above the altar shows the Madonna with the Infant Jesus surrounded by SS. Sebastian, Francis, and Clare of Assisi.*

The monasteries of the Carmelites

Named after Mount Carmel in Palestine, the Carmelite order, which combines eremitism and contemplation with active pastoral care and academic study, was given a number of major monastery complexes in Portugal. The monastery church of Igreja do Carmo in Lisbon, completed by 1423, has been left in its ruined state as a memorial to the devastating earthquake of 1755. The construction of the monastery and church, once Lisbon's largest place of worship and the only one built exclusively in the Gothic style, dates back to a vow made by national hero and royal military commander Nuno Álvares Pereira (1360–1431), who secured Portugal's independence from Castile at the Battle of Aljubarrota in 1385. In 1422 he entered the monastery as a Carmelite friar and died there in 1431, having acquired an aura of sanctity.

The monastery church was built on sloping ground. In order to create a level structure, the constituent architectural elements needed to be of varying heights. The west end of the complex, with its impressive door, has lost its roof, but some of the ceiling ribs remain, making the building look like an enormous skeleton. The less badly damaged eastern portion gives a better impression of what the complex would once have been like.

The church of Santa Maria delle Grazie at Soncino (Lombardy) was constructed for the Carmelite monastery there between 1501 and 1528, and in 1531/2 decorated throughout with frescoes by Giulio Campi and the brothers Bernardino and Francesco Carminati. Regarded as a good example of Lombard Renaissance architecture, it houses a sculpture of Our Gracious Lady and has a Lady chapel and two further chapels. From 1536 onwards it also served as the private chapel and burial chapel of the noble Stampa family.

In 1621, a group of monks belonging to the strict Carmelite congregation known as the Discalced (Barefoot) Carmelites, withdrew to the wilderness that is now the nature reserve near Benicàssim (Valencia, Spain). By 1694 they had established a monastery known as Desert de les Palmes, consisting of a church ringed by dwarf palms with hermitages dotting the surrounding area. The new monastery, still in use today, was built in the 18th century in the immediate vicinity of the old one. Since 1896 it has financed itself through the production of its popular herbal liqueur "Licor Carmelitano."

*Left above: a side chapel of the church of Santa Maria delle Grazie at the **Carmelite monastery of Soncino** (Lombardy). The construction and decoration of the church were sponsored by the powerful Sforza family, who were the rulers of Milan.*

*Left below: the new **Carmelite convent of Desert de les Palmes near Benicàssim** (Spain), which is still in use, dates from the 18th century and is located in the middle of a nature reserve.*

*Opposite page: the freestanding arcading of **Igreja do Carmo in Lisbon**, a memorial to the earthquake of 1755. The side wings now contain archaeological collections.*

Charterhouses

The Carthusians, one of the strictest of all Christian monastic orders, were founded by St. Bruno of Cologne (c. 1030–1101) in 1084, when he and six companions established the Grande Chartreuse in the mountains near Grenoble. This was to serve as the mother house and architectural model for the order, which to this day combines eremitism with a rudimentary form of communal living. Bruno was soon summoned by Pope Urban to Italy, where he founded the order's second house at La Torre (Calabria).

The Grande Chartreuse displays the layout that all later houses were to follow. The monks came together for Divine Office in the plain, single-nave stone church and assembled at set times in the chapter house and refectory. Opening off the cloister were the monks' sparsely furnished single cells. These were built of wood and had individual gardens which were separated from the neighboring cells by a high wall.

In 1132 the original Chartreuse was destroyed by an avalanche and rebuilt just over 1 mile (2 kilometers) to the south. The new complex burned down a total of eight times and had to be repeatedly rebuilt. Most of the existing buildings date from the 17th century, although there are a number of individual elements that are older. The monastery was dissolved in 1903 but Carthusian monks have been living here again since 1940.

One of the biggest and most important charterhouses, at Gaming (Austria), was founded in 1330 by Duke Albrecht II of Austria and bore the name "Marienthron" (Mary's Throne). It was a double monastery with 24 monks instead of the originally prescribed 12. Consecrated in 1342, this charterhouse was the beneficiary of substantial endowments, particularly after the interment of its founder here in 1358.

In 1453 the monastery church with its original rib vault was given a Late Gothic cap vault and side chapels. Further buildings such as the prelature were added after 1585 and the library was completed between 1702 and 1739. Under Nikolaus Kempf III (prior 1451–58), Gaming developed into a center of learning and boasted more monks than any other Carthusian house. The interior of the monastery church was reworked in the Baroque style between 1742 and 1746. While the walls still correspond to the Carthusian ideal of simplicity, the ceiling and cupola are magnificently decorated. Gaming was dissolved by state decree in 1782, but the monastery buildings were maintained and carefully restored by subsequent owners.

Above: the church of the Carthusian monastery at Gaming presents a rather plain exterior to which its slender pointed tower adds an element of gracefulness.

Opposite page: the mother house of the Carthusian order, the Grande Chartreuse near Grenoble, lies in a valley surrounded by precipitous cliffs. Since 1755 the monastery has been renowned for its "Chartreuse" liqueur, which is made from over 130 herbs and spices.

Left: in contrast to its magnificent ceiling, the walls of the interior of the monastery church at Gaming have been kept simple and unadorned.

The monasteries of the Augustinians and Bridgettines

The Augustinians lived in poverty and brotherly harmony, but also with mutual admonition and assistance in accordance with the Rule of St. Augustine of Hippo, a preeminent doctor of the Church. In 1276 the Augustinians were given the church of St. Philippi und Jacobi in Erfurt, built in 1131, and began work converting it into a monastery the following year. The monastery church received its stained-glass windows between 1310 and 1340, and by 1518 the nave, tower, cloister, and other monastery buildings were completed.

The young Martin Luther (1483–1546) entered the monastery in 1505, and was ordained as a priest there in 1507 before leaving for Wittenberg four years later. In 1522 the monastery joined Luther's Reform movement and was secularized in 1559.

In 1142 Bishop Hartmann of Brixen founded the monastery of Neustift (Novacella) as a chapter of Augustinian canons in an inhospitable hollow near Brixen, Bressanone in Tyrol, Italy. Although the monastery had to do battle with the bishops of Brixen—and the counts of Tyrol for its freedoms and independent jurisdiction, it became so powerful as a result of endowments that by 1500 it already owned 542 farms, 49 houses, 5 mills, 82 vineyards, 58 meadows, and 76 arable fields.

Vadstena Monastery was laid out in 1346 as the mother house of the Bridgettine order founded by Bridget of Sweden (1303–73). A chatelaine and mother of eight children, Bridget lost her husband in 1344 and received her calling to found an order five years later. As a Christian visionary, she acquired considerable political influence.

Built between 1369 and 1430, and enlarged several times, the aisled Gothic church of blue-gray limestone was kept emphatically simple and unadorned in accordance with Bridget's instructions. As the result of numerous endowments, the monastery became Sweden's biggest landowner and survived the Reformation, which started to sweep through the land in 1523, until 1595. In 1374, Bridget was succeeded as abbess by her daughter St. Catherine of Sweden (1331/2–82), who brought her mother's relics back from Rome where she had died. Vadstena immediately became an important center of pilgrimage.

*Above: the **church** of **St. Birgitta at Vadstena Monastery**, the mother house of the Bridgettine order. In Sweden the church is known as the "Blåkyrkan" (Blue Church) because of its blue-gray stone façade.*

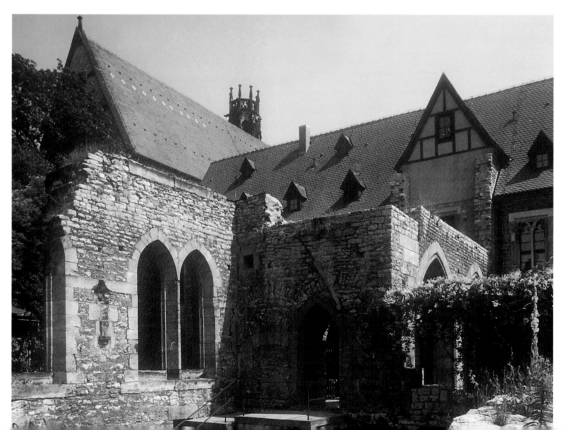

*Left: the **Augustinerkloster in Erfurt**, where for six years Martin Luther was a monk. In 1561 the monastery was transformed into a school and orphanage and since 1996 has accommodated a community of sisters belonging to the Protestant Casteller Ring order.*

69

The Castles of the Knightly Orders

*Above: a stone figure of a Knight Templar at the **Castle of Tomar**.*

The religious orders of knights, founded originally to protect pilgrims and defend the Holy Land after its conquest during the Crusades, became powerful landowners in Europe too. In accordance with the ideal of soldier monks, most of the members of these orders resided in castles belonging to their order.

The castles of the Knights Templar

In 1160 the Order of the Knights Templar established its headquarters in England on a site known as "Middle Temple" in the heart of London. The first structure to be built was the fortress-like Round Church, consecrated in 1185. Inspired by the Holy Sepulcher of Christ in Jerusalem, the church contains marble effigies of nine famous knights of the order. The adjacent rectangular chancel, whose roof is supported by columns of black marble, was completed by 1240. The Templars grew so powerful that in 1307 Philip the Fair, king of France (reigned 1285–1314), initiated a trial on spurious charges of heresy and forced Pope Clement V to dissolve the order in 1312. The last grand master of the Templars, Jacques de Molay, was burned at the stake two years later. The Temple in London was then transformed into a college for barristers attached to the courts in London, until its appropriation for the Crown by Henry VIII in 1540.

*Above: the **Convento de Cristo in Tomar**. The former Templar castle was the beneficiary of generous endowments, in particular from King Manuel I (reigned 1495–1521), who as crown prince was grand master of the Order of Christ.*

*Opposite page: the Round Church and Chancel of **Temple Church in London**. It was here that England's barons forced the king to recognize the Magna Carta in 1215.*

One of the most famous Templar castles is the Convento de Cristo in the Portuguese town of Tomar. In the 12th century, Alfonso I of Portugal (reigned 1139–85) invited the experienced knights into his kingdom to help with the Wars of Reconquest (*Reconquista*) against the Moors. The castle was begun in 1160 and the foundations of the first cloister laid in 1162. The Romanesque chapel takes the form of a 16-sided polygon with round windows and a belfry. Its octagonal inner ground plan recalls the Holy Sepulcher in Jerusalem.

Portugal was the only country to protect the Templars from persecution in 1307. However, following the order's dissolution, the Tomar castle complex was given, in 1319, to the newly founded Order of Christ. In the years up to 1618, the complex was enlarged a number of times and the number of cloisters increased to no fewer than eight. The more recent buildings, dating from after 1510, were erected in the Manueline style, decorated with stone rope moldings and coral motifs—notably the side arched portal between the original Templar building and the longitudinal Manueline structure. Numerous legends have sprung up concerning Tomar's connection with the Holy Grail, which is supposed to have been in the possession of the Templars, and the allegedly immeasurable wealth of the order.

A bastion that withstood the Ottoman siege of 1565: Fort St. Angelo, headquarters of the grand master of the Knights Hospitaller, situated on a promontory of Malta.

The castles of the Knights Hospitaller (Knights of Malta)

The stronghold that previously occupied the site of what is probably the most famous castle of any military order in the Middle East, the extremely well-fortified Krak des Chevaliers in Syria, was built by the emir of Hims in 1031 and given the name Hisn al-Akrad (Castle of the Kurds). It was conquered by Christian knights in 1099 during the First Crusade to Jerusalem. In 1110 it became part of the County of Tripoli (a Crusader state) and was ceded to the Knights Hospitaller in 1142.

Following two earthquakes, the Hospitallers embarked on a large-scale reconstruction in 1170, adding a main tower, a chapel, a monumental gateway, a massive curtain wall with three towers, and a moat on three sides. After 1202 the stronghold was further reinforced through the construction of round towers, scree slopes to help protect against earthquakes and walls up to 26 feet (8 meters) thick. In 1250 an outer wall was added. By 1267 the Egyptian Mamluk sultan Baibar (reigned 1260–77) had captured the surrounding castles and laid siege to Krak with trebuchets. In April 1271 the Knights Hospitaller eventually surrendered.

In 1309, after their expulsion from the Holy Land, the Hospitallers conquered Rhodes from the Byzantines and made it their new headquarters. In 1522 they were forced to leave the island by the Ottomans and were given the islands of Malta and Gozo in fiefdom by Emperor Charles V. They immediately fortified the two islands with a ring of strongholds and citadels. That same year the

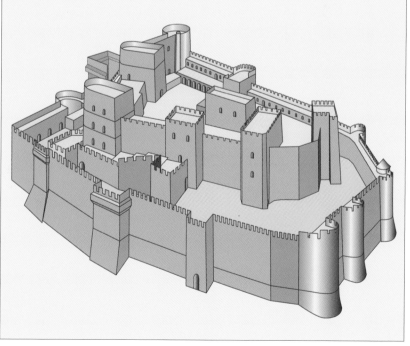

Above: the inner precinct of Krak des Chevaliers in Syria contained a number of halls in the High Gothic style. Having been unsuccessfully besieged by Sultan Saladin in 1188, the fortress was eventually captured by Sultan Baibar in 1271.

Below: the Knights Hospitaller's castle of Krak des Chevaliers in Syria. It is shown here as it was around 1290 after having been extended by the Mamluks (based on a 19th-century reconstructive drawing).

knights started work expanding a small castle located on the promontory of Birgu (today Vittoriosa) on the north coast of Malta into a major fort, which they named St. Angelo. This was to become the headquarters of the grand master of the order and also accommodated the house of the castellan and the order's chapel of St. Anne.

In 1565 the Knights Hospitaller repelled a siege by the Ottoman fleet under the command of the notorious corsair Turgut Reis, who was killed during the campaign. In March 1566 the knights founded the city of Valletta (named after Jean Parisot de la Vallette, grand master 1557–68). In 1798 the Hospitallers capitulated to Napoleon's forces, who expelled them from the island. A purely religious branch of the order, the Sovereign Military Order of Malta, was established in Rome in 1834.

*The **castle and cathedral of Marienwerder** (Kwidzyn)— fine examples of 13th- and 14th-century Brick Gothic.*

The castles of the Teutonic Order

After losing its possessions in the Holy Land, the Teutonic Order was given Marienburg near Danzig (Gdansk) as its new headquarters and seat of its grand master (until 1454). The imposing Marienburg Castle was the center of the German colonization of East Prussia, Poland, and Livonia. It comprises three distinct architectural ensembles, the oldest of which, completed in 1280, is the main castle, consisting of a fort-like four-wing structure with chapter house. The other constituent elements are the knights' accommodation and a chapel. Between 1309 and 1400 a Gothic tower house (donjon) was built onto the central castle to serve as the grand master's palace, as well as two light and airy halls designed to be used as summer and winter refectories with star vaults supported by a single slender granite column in the middle of the room. The outer castle, comprising the outer wall, chapel of St. Lawrence, commanderie, and pier bridge, was more or less complete by 1309. Following the defeat of the order at Tannenberg in 1410, Marienburg Castle withstood a siege by Polish and Lithuanian troops before being brought under Polish sovereignty in 1455.

Other castles belonging to the Teutonic Order also became centers for the German colonization of Baltic Prussia (now Poland). The castle and town of Marienwerder (Kwidzyn), on which work started in 1232/4, became the diocesan town of Pomesania, one of four bishoprics in the hands of the Teutonic Order in the east. The cathedral was built between 1343 and 1384. All that now remains of the castle are two wings, three corner towers, and a two-story cloister.

Heilsberg (today Lidzbark Warminski in Poland) was built by the Teutonic Order in 1240 and was made the seat of another of the bishoprics administered by the knights, that of Ermland. Its prince-bishops held onto Heilsberg Castle even after the city had come under Polish sovereignty in 1466, and it remained in their possession until 1772. The castle's outer ward, walls and moat were built between 1350 and 1400 as part of the defenses against the Lithuanians. After 1590 the complex was extended several times— through the addition of a palace known as the "Cardinal's Chambers" and later a "Middle Palace" on the south side (1666), for example. Subsequent alterations included a park in the Rococo style.

Above: **Heilsberg Castle** *(Lidzbark Warminski) was built by the Teutonic Order after the Baltic Prussians had briefly reoccupied Heilsberg between 1261 and 1273.*

Below: **Marienburg Castle** *near Danzig (Gdansk), the headquarters of the Teutonic Order, is one of the largest and most impressive Brick Gothic buildings in Europe.*

Beguinages and female piety

Lay communities of beguines—the origins of the name are not known for certain; according to one legend it derives from St. Begga—and beghards, their male counterparts, started to emerge at the beginning of the 13th century. The lay sisters and brothers of these communities, which in many respects resembled religious orders, devoted themselves to the care of the sick, the poor, and the "fallen."

Particularly common in the Netherlands and Flanders, these communities generally came into being through the joining of forces and resources by numbers of unmarried women and widows of all ranks, and often developed into influential societies. In Amsterdam, for example—as well as Breda, Antwerp, Bruges, Ghent, Leuven, Mechlin, and Turnhout—beguinages sprang up in the center of town (though separated off by walls or moats) and consisted of a number of small dwelling houses plus chapel, assembly room, infirmary, and mistress's house grouped around an inner courtyard planted out as a kitchen or ornamental garden. The model was copied in other European countries and some of the beguinages continued to be inhabited into the 19th century.

Until the dawning of the modern age, the established church generally took a skeptical view of these independent religious lay movements that operated outside its control. Before long, many of them came to be suspected of heresy under the dogma *extra ecclesiam nulla salus* (no salvation outside the church).

*Beguines' dwellings in the **beguinage at Kortrijk** (Belgium) founded in 1238. Forty-two houses dating from the 13th century survive. A further 40 homes in the Baroque style were added in the 17th century.*

*Right: the chapel of St. Spiritus at the **beguine hospital in Havelberg, Brandenburg**. This rectangular brick building with high Gothic window niches was completed in 1390.*

Women's religious orders (and branches of orders) in the true sense were always subject to particularly strict control. While the Church awarded due recognition to great mystics such as Hildegard of Bingen (1098–1179), Catherine of Siena (1347–80) and Teresa of Ávila (1515–82), it required the female branches of "active" men's orders— the Franciscans or Carmelites, for example—to play a purely contemplative role. Women's orders had to fight long and hard for the right to perform "active" Christian service in public, for example the preaching of the faith by Dominican sisters. Most female monastics "emancipated" themselves within the context of caring for the sick and destitute and later through teaching, an area in which they often played a leading role.

Right: the Benedictine nun and mystic Hildegard of Bingen (1098–1179) was one of the few women of the Middle Ages to preach in public (painting in the abbey of St. Hildegard in Rüdesheim, Germany).

Monasteries of the Renaissance

The monastery of **St. Jerome in Belém**, *Lisbon, measures 984 feet (300 meters) from end to end. The church alone is 295 feet (90 meters) long and its cupola rises to a height of 82 feet (25 meters).*

For the Catholic Church the Late Renaissance was dominated by the Counter-Reformation, a process of inner renewal in response to the Reformation. New orders, above all the Jesuits and Capuchins, dedicated themselves to the spiritual welfare of the general public, and announced their presence in the centers of towns and cities by creating magnificent façades.

The life of the Church was revived by numerous reformers. One such was the Spanish mystic, saint, and doctor of the Church, Teresa of Ávila (1515–82), who founded 17 convents of the Discalced (Barefoot) Carmelites by herself and a further 32 monasteries in collaboration with her companion, the mystic St. John of the Cross (1542–91).

A new field of activity for the religious orders was missionary work in the New World, which had recently been conquered by Spain and Portugal. Numerous religious houses, such as the Augustinian monastery of Yuriria in Mexico, were erected in the Spanish colonial style in Central and South America.

Perhaps the best example of an individual style of architecture is the monastery of St. Jerome (Mosteiro dos Jerónimos) in Lisbon, founded by Manuel I (reigned 1495–1521) in 1500. The Portuguese king, nicknamed "the Fortunate," made Portugal a world sea power and created the Manueline style of architecture that combined elements of the Late Gothic and Renaissance styles with maritime motifs such as decorative elements inspired by ship's ropes.

The monastery complex was built between 1502 and 1571. The monastery church, with its richly decorated limestone façade, was completed in 1544 and has a two-story cloister that gives onto a refectory decorated with glazed tiles. Manuel's son João III (reigned 1521–57) added a choir. The main door is decorated with depictions of St. Jerome and Portuguese kings and seafarers.

Badly damaged by Napoleon's troops in 1807, the monastery remained the seat of the Order of St. Jerome until 1834. King Manuel I and a number of his successors are buried in the crypt along with various Portuguese explorers including Vasco da Gama (1469–1524).

*Above: the upper portion of the chancel of the **monastery church of St. Jerome in Lisbon** is a good example of Portugal's highly individual Manueline style during the transition from Late Gothic to Renaissance.*

*Below: a statue of Teresa of Ávila, founder of the Discalced Carmelites, in front of the **convent of the Holy Incarnation (Santa Maria de la Encarnación) in Ávila**, where the saint was for a long time prioress.*

Dominican monasteries of the Renaissance

As the spiritual spearhead of the battle against heresy during the late medieval period, the Dominicans received special support from rulers. In 1388, John I of Portugal (reigned 1385–1433) presented them with the monastery of Santa Maria da Vitória (Our Lady of the Victory) in Batalha.

The aisled monastery church with transept and cloister on the north side was completed in 1437. The cloister with pump house was embellished with slender arcading in the Manueline style around 1500. On the eastern side of the cloister is the chapter house with a star vault with no central support, one of the largest of its type constructed in the Late Middle Ages. In 1470 the monastery complex, of uncommon flamboyance for a mendicant order, was given another small cloister in the more customary simple and sober Dominican style.

Construction of the Founder's Chapel (Capela do Fundador), a mortuary chapel for John I and other members of the royal house, began in 1426. John's son Duarte (reigned 1433–38) expanded the complex through the addition of another chapel that was to remain unfinished (Capelas Imperfeitas). Further additions were made in the 18th century.

The Dominicans' missionary monasteries in the New World, such as Santo Domingo in Lima (Peru) or Santo Domingo de Guzmán in Oaxaca (Mexico), were also richly appointed. The monastery at Oaxaca was built between 1552 and around 1650. The monks, who had already been settled here for nearly 80 years, moved into the still unfinished building in 1608 when their old monastery was destroyed in an earthquake.

The west front of this monastery church displays a monumentality typical of the Renaissance, although in this case the solidity is justified by Oaxaca's vulnerability to powerful earthquakes, 22 of which shook the city between 1696 and 1999, repeatedly causing damage.

The Dominican monastery was dissolved in 1857 and the church used as a cavalry depot before being restored to its original purpose in 1902. The monastery was handed back to the Dominicans in 1938 and was converted into a museum with attached botanical garden in 1993.

*Above: the cupola of the **monastery church of Santo Domingo de Guzmán in Oaxaca**, which soars above the gilded altar wall with its statue of the Madonna.*

*Left: the **monastery church of Santo Domingo de Guzmán in Oaxaca** possesses a massive Renaissance façade with an entrance portal 85 feet (26 meters) high flanked by two 115-feet-high towers, a method of construction designed to withstand earthquakes.*

*Right: as the burial place of the Portuguese monarchy, the **Dominican monastery of Batalha** was uncommonly richly appointed for a monastery of a mendicant order.*

Jesuit monasteries in Europe and the New World

Not only was the Jesuit order the motor behind the Catholic Counter-Reformation, it also played a pioneering role architecturally. The order's mother house, Il Gèsu in Rome, was built between 1568 and 1584 (and occupied by the Jesuits from 1575) to plans by the Italian architect Giacomo Barozzi da Vignola (1507–73). In terms of its construction and façade design it pointed the way forward for Jesuit churches during the transition from Renaissance to Baroque.

The nave has a barrel vault with a well-lit crossing dome and is flanked by lower-ceilinged chapels. The interior, comprising a central space with a series of subsidiary structures, was designed to accord with the new liturgy established at the Council of Trent (1545–63). Between 1668 and 1673 the interior was refurbished in the Baroque style with a preponderance of gold. The ceiling fresco above the nave depicts *The Triumph of the Name of Jesus*. The façade is divided clearly into two stories while the roofs of the side chapels terminate in volutes (scrolls).

In 1556 Ferdinand I (Holy Roman Emperor 1558–64) invited the Jesuits to the university city of Prague to act as a counterweight to Protestantism, which was gaining the upper hand throughout Bohemia. The order was given to the Collegium Clementinum (in the Old Town), which became the Catholic University in 1616. Work started on the college church of St. Salvator in 1578. Following the completion of the choir (the oldest part), the basilica was added in 1601.

After defeating the Protestants in the Thirty Years War (1621), Emperor Ferdinand III gave the Jesuits Charles University, which merged with the Clementinum in 1654.

Between 1653 and 1726, the church and the Clementinum were remodeled in the Baroque style, the complex was expanded, and a library and observatory added. The college developed into a bastion of scientific learning. After 1775 it became renowned for its regularly conducted and recorded observations of the weather.

When the Jesuits were suppressed in 1773, college and church passed into the hands of the state and were later annexed to Charles University. Since 2004, the church of St. Saviour has been the seat of an academic parish.

*Above: drawing (based on
the photograph of a model)
illustrating the design of the
façade of the Jesuit mother
house Il Gesù in Rome, which
became a model for many
other church fronts.*

*Right: the façade of the
Jesuit mother house **Il Gesù
in Rome** set a style that
was copied by other Jesuit
churches. The lower story
consists of five pairs of
pilasters (non-load-bearing
demi-columns) while the
narrower upper story tapers
upward into a triangular
pediment.*

Within Europe, the Jesuits took a particular interest in Poland, where Protestantism had gained a foothold. The Jesuit theologian and counter-reformer Piotr Skarga (1536–1612) was made court preacher to Sigismund III in 1588. Twelve years later he persuaded the Polish king to found the Jesuit church of SS. Peter and Paul in Kraków. Modeled on the mother house of Il Gesù in Rome, the church was completed by 1635 to designs by court architect Giovanni Trevano (died 1644), and is the earliest example of Early Baroque architecture in Kraków.

From the 16th century up to its expulsion in 1767, the Jesuit order played a leading role in the mission to the indigenous peoples of the New World, above all in the territories of the New World administered by Spain. In Cuzco in Peru, work started on the convent church of La Compañía de Jesús, located opposite the cathedral, in 1571. Destroyed in a severe earthquake in 1650, the church was rebuilt over the subsequent two decades and given an impressive new façade with twin towers. Inside, the main altars (1670, architect Diego Martínez de Oviedo), which are covered with gold leaf, radiate a particular splendor that takes up the sun motif of the local indigenous population. In 1585 the Jesuits arrived in Córdoba in Argentina. In 1599 they were given a plot of land which they turned into the center of their mission along the "Jesuit Trail," a series of settlements in the Córdoba region. The Jesuit block (Manzana de los Jesuitas) in Córdoba comprised a number of monasteries and churches as well as a university (1613).

In 1590 the inhabitants of Rio de Janeiro in Brazil invited a group of Benedictine monks to the town. Here they founded the abbey of São Bento and erected the church of Nossa Senhora de Montserrat (1617–69), whose interior, furnished in the 18th century with magnificent chapels, wood carvings and inlaid goldwork, contrasts strongly with its simple façade. Alongside various social facilities, the monastery complex, which was enlarged on several occasions, most recently in 1880, now incorporates Benedictine theological university of Brazil and a publishing house.

*Opposite page: the **Jesuit church of SS. Peter and Paul in Kraków**. In the 18th century, Late Baroque sculptures of the 12 apostles were erected in front of the main entrance. The preacher Piotr Skarga is buried in the crypt.*

*Left: around 45 monks still live in the **Benedictine abbey of São Bento in Rio de Janeiro**, the third-oldest monastery on the American continent.*

*Right below: the **church of La Compañía de Jesús**, the church of the Jesuit College of Cuzco, with its double-tower façade. A painting inside the church commemorates the marriage of the nephew of Ignatius of Loyola to the niece of Tupac Amaru, the last of the Inca rulers, in 1572.*

*Right above: the second courtyard of the **Jesuit establishment of Santa Catalina** in Argentina, a filiation of the Jesuit center in the city of Córdoba.*

Above: the former Franciscan monastery in Plzeň, subsequently remodeled in the Baroque style, is now the diocesan museum. The cloister houses a collection of sculpture from the Gothic, Renaissance, and Baroque eras.

Franciscan and Capuchin monasteries of the Renaissance

The monastery of Madonna del Sasso, a popular place of pilgrimage, is located on a hilltop above Locarno. It was founded after the Virgin Mary appeared to Franciscan monk Bartolomeo Piatti d'Ivrea in 1480. The chapels of Santa Maria Avvocata and the Pietà were erected between 1485 and 1487, along with a small Franciscan convent (Casa del Padre) that was expanded before long into an extensive monastery complex.

In 1502 a church of the Annunciation (Santa Maria Annunciata) was built at the foot of the hill, from where a footpath incorporating the 12 Stations of the Passion of Christ leads up to the summit. In 1616 the chapel of Santa Maria Avvocata was elevated to the church of Santa Maria Assunta (known as Madonna del Sasso).

After a gradual decline, the monastery was dissolved in 1848 and the entire complex handed to the Capuchins, who substantially expanded and restored it as a place of pilgrimage in 1890 and subsequently a number of times between 1912 and 1984.

Another place of pilgrimage closely associated with the Capuchins is Altötting in Bavaria. Following the secularization of Bavaria in 1802, a congregation of around 150 Capuchin monks moved into the Franciscan monastery of St. Anna, founded by the prince-bishop of Regensburg in 1654, in order to look after the pilgrims. Konrad von Parzham (1818–94), a Capuchin lay brother who was canonized in 1934, arrived in 1849 and served as gatekeeper for 41 years. The monastery church and monastery were renamed after St. Konrad in 1953 and 1961 respectively.

At the same time, the Capuchins were presented with the Jesuit church of St. Magdalena, which was built in 1593 and remodeled by Jesuit brother Thomas Troyer in the Baroque style between 1697 and 1700. The church's splendid side altars (1712/3) and high altar (1795) were added later.

Plzeň (Czech Republic) was founded in 1295 and its Franciscan monastery around the same time. The city became a center of the Hussite movement in 1417 before becoming Catholic again three years later. It subsequently suffered a long siege by the Hussites which was not lifted until 1434. During these upheavals the monastery was twice burned down and rebuilt. The monastery church of St. Maria possesses a Late Gothic cloister and a 15th-century chapel of St. Barbara decorated with frescoes.

*Left: the **Capuchin church of St. Magdalena and the Gnadenkapelle at Altötting**. The Gnadenkapelle (Chapel of Grace) contains a famous "Black Madonna". Altötting became a place of pilgrimage in 1489 when a child who was thought to be dead made a miraculous recovery.*

*Opposite page: the initially **Franciscan monastery complex of Madonna del Sasso**, which nestles on a hilltop overlooking Locarno and Lago Maggiore, lost its original simplicity when the church of the Assumption (Santa Maria Assunta) was given a neo-Renaissance façade in 1890.*

The Capuchin cult of the dead

A strange phenomenon that developed during the transition from the Renaissance to the Baroque, and one which can strike modern observers as somewhat macabre, is the cult of the dead, which was practiced predominantly by the Capuchin order. The monks collected the bones of their deceased brethren and arranged them artistically in order to serve as graphic representations of the transitory nature of earthly existence and to exhort the living to remember their mortality (Latin: *memento mori*).

A particularly impressive example of this practice can be viewed at the Capuchin church of Santa Maria della Concezione dei Cappuccini (built 1626–31) in Rome. Beginning in 1628, the Capuchin cardinal Antonio Barberini (1569–1646), brother of Pope Urban VIII (reigned 1623–44), arranged to have the remains of deceased members of the order collected for display in the church crypt. By 1870 the bones of over 4,000 monks, including a number of complete skeletons still wearing the habit of their order, had been stacked up in artistic formations. The crypt was divided into five dimly lit chapels and inspired writers such as the marquis de Sade, Mark Twain, and Nathaniel Hawthorn in the 18th and 19th centuries.

Something similar was done by monks in the crypt of the Capuchin church (commenced 1651) of the Holy Cross in Brno (Czech Republic), where deceased brethren can be seen at rest, clothed in their habits. Perhaps the best-known Capuchin catacombs are located in Palermo beneath Sicily's first Capuchin monastery (commenced 1534). In 1599 a crypt was dug beneath the main altar of the monastery church. Mainly monks (up to 1671) and later citizens of Palermo too (up to 1881) were set out in a series of corridors ordered by social group (monks, priests, men, women, profession).

The monks mummified the dead in drying chambers made of tuff, which drew out all the fluids from the bodies, and then in the sun before clothing them in their vestments. Of a total of 8,000 mummies, some 1,200 remain on display, including the very first, that of Fra. Silvestro da Gubbio, which was put on view in 1599.

*Above: the mummy of a priest clothed in his vestments in the "Corridor of the Priests" in the **Capuchin catacombs in Palermo**.*

*Opposite page: an artistic arrangement of monks' bones adorning the second chapel of the crypt of **Santa Maria della Concezione dei Cappucini in Rome**. A plaque exhorts the living to remember that "What you are now, we were once. What we are now, you will soon be."*

*Right: cult of the dead: this photograph from the 1950s shows a Capuchin monk dusting the bones of his co-brethren in **Santa Maria della Concezione**.*

Baroque Monasteries

The Baroque and ensuing Rococo eras saw many monasteries and orders at the height of their power and prosperity. Impressive monastery churches were furnished with magnificent main and side altars, enormous ceiling frescoes and altar paintings, and highly detailed wood carvings and statues. Catholicism during the Baroque era presented itself in an overtly sensuous way through large gestures and striking symbolism.

Benedictine abbeys of the Baroque era

After the Thirty Years War (1618–48), Niederaltaich Abbey, dedicated to St. Maurice and founded by Duke Odilo of Bavaria in 741, experienced a significant improvement in its economic fortunes that enabled Joscio Hamberger (abbot 1700–39) in the next generation to undertake a complete

renovation of the monastery complex in the Baroque style. Most importantly, the monastery's aisled hall church in the Gothic style was transformed into a light-filled Baroque edifice. Dissolved in 1803, the monastery was reoccupied by Benedictine monks in 1918 and since 1949 has once again enjoyed the status of self-governing abbey.

Weltenburg Abbey, situated above a loop of the River Danube near Kelheim, was the last monastery to be founded in Bavaria by Irish monks. Despite having been plundered a number of times (most recently during the Thirty Years War), Weltenburg Abbey experienced an improvement in its fortunes at the beginning of the 18th century. Maurus Bächl I (abbot 1713–43) commissioned the rebuilding of the entire complex in the Baroque style. The abbey church (1716–39), designed by the Brothers Asam, consists of a porch, an oval main church (with an open cupola supported by eight marble columns), and a rectangular chancel (presbytery). Secularized in 1803, Weltenburg was reoccupied by monks in 1842, becoming a self-governing abbey in 1913.

Ettal Abbey was founded by Emperor Louis in 1330. After its church was all but destroyed by lightning in 1744, it was rebuilt in the High Baroque style by members of the Wessobrunn School, which played a leading role in monastic architecture in Germany at that time. Dissolved in 1803, Ettal was reoccupied by Benedictine monks in 1900 and became an abbey again in 1907.

*Above: the **abbey church at Ettal**, built in the High Baroque style by architect and stuccoist Joseph Schmuzer (1683–1752) of the Wessobrunn School.*

*Left: **Weltenburg Abbey**, which is under constant threat of being flooded by the Danube. The Baroque abbey church exploits the contrast between light and dark to dramatic effect and contains a famous ceiling fresco,* The Church Triumphant, *painted by Cosmas Daman Asam in 1721.*

*Opposite page: the Baroque **church of Niederaltaich Abbey**. The nave was embellished with massive columns, ceiling frescoes, gilded wood carvings, and a high altar.*

The Baroque monasteries in Austria enjoyed particular support from the Habsburg emperors. Stift Göttweig, for example, which was founded in 1083, was given to the Benedictines in 1094 and became self-governing in 1401. The nave of the abbey church and the castle belonging to the monastery complex survive from the 12th century and the Late Gothic choir, crypt, and cloister from the 15th.

After two fires (in 1580 and 1718), Gottfried Bessel (abbot 1714–49) initiated a thorough rebuilding to designs by the famous Baroque architect Johann Lucas von Hildebrandt (1668–1745), only two-thirds of whose plans were ultimately realized. The abbey church—whose façade was completed in 1750 and whose nave possesses eight side chapels—had already been given a high altar, pulpit, and organ cabinet in 1639. The large altarpiece dating from 1694 depicts the *Reception of the Virgin Mary into Heaven*. Abbot Gottfried Bessel was also the rector of Vienna University and, during his incumbency, Göttweig became an important seat of learning with a particular focus on literature, history, and the natural sciences.

Melk Abbey, built in 1089 on a site overlooking the River Danube, had already become self-governing in 1122 and had been richly endowed by the dukes of Austria of the Babenberg dynasty, whose mortuary chapel was located there. Melk's precious library, however, was destroyed in a fire, along with the abbey and church, in 1297. Under Nikolaus Seyringer (abbot 1418–25), the abbey became the center of the Melk Reform movement, which embraced a stricter form of monastic discipline and started to prosper from around 1580.

Abbot Berthold Dietmayr (in office between 1700 and 1739) undertook a Baroque remodeling of the abbey under the direction of architect Jakob Prandtauer. This resulted in Austria's largest Baroque monastery complex, with a principal axis 1,050 feet (320 meters) long. After a fire in 1738, Melk was immediately rebuilt. Passing through the entrance arch and Benedictine Hall, visitors enter the trapezoid Prelate's Court providing access to the imposing Imperial Wing and Marble Hall via the Imperial Staircase.

Below: the extensive complex of **Melk Abbey and its church** (drawing based on a wooden model).

*Above: the ceiling vault of the main room of the **monastery library at Metten**, conceived as an independent cosmos, is "borne aloft" by pairs of atlantes. In the adjoining rooms, the same function is performed by angels.*

*Right: books in the library at **Melk Abbey**, uniformly bound and lettered in brown and gold. The collection extends over two stories.*

Monastery libraries: the jewel in the crown

The scriptoria of the early monasteries had already been bastions of learning and book arts. In them manuscripts were copied, translated, and artistically illuminated. Until the emergence of the universities in the Late Middle Ages, the book collections of the monasteries were the most important libraries in the Western world.

In addition to theology, philosophy, literature, and history, during the modern age monks also turned to the natural sciences (such as geology, zoology, and botany), as well as the systematic mapping of the surrounding area. In the large Baroque monasteries, the designing

of the library became the second most important task after the planning of the abbey church. Allegorical frescoes and statues celebrated the coming together of faith and learning under one roof. The monasteries were stressing—while asserting the supremacy of faith—that there was no contradiction between the two.

The library of the Benedictine abbey of Metten (1722–26) was designed as a main room with two side rooms and decorated with an allegorical scheme representing the library as a "temple of wisdom." The ceiling fresco of the main room celebrates the primacy of divine revelation over all human knowledge. With nearly 200,000 volumes, Metten's library is one of the largest of any monastery. The ceiling frescoes by Paul Troger in the two main rooms

of the library at Melk depict faith and the four cardinal virtues: faith, temperance, fortitude, and justice. In 1997, a fragment of a 13th-century copy of the *Nibelungenlied* was discovered among Melk's collection of around 100,000 books (including 1,800 manuscripts from the 9th century and 750 incunabula, or first editions, dating from before 1500). The library at the Benedictine abbey of Admont has a collection of 200,000 books including 1,400 volumes from the Middle Ages and possesses the largest main room of any monastic library in the world (230 x 46 feet/70 x 14 meters). Its ceiling is made up of seven domes and its sculptures represent the *Four Last Things* (death, the Last Judgment, heaven, and hell). Its frescoes celebrate divine revelation and the stages of human knowledge.

*Completed in 1776, the library at **Admont Abbey** is the world's largest monastic library and was once referred to as the eighth wonder of the world. It is illuminated by 48 windows and its decorative scheme symbolizes the conjunction of faith and enlightenment.*

Cistercian abbeys of the Baroque era

*The **library at Stift Zwettl** was built by the architect Joseph Munggenast (1680–1741) between 1730 and 1732. Its opulent ceiling frescoes are the work of Paul Troger. Munggenast was responsible for the design of the entire Baroque complex at Zwettl Abbey.*

Stift Zwettl in the Waldviertel region of Lower Austria was founded by Count Hadamar I von Kuenring in 1138 and occupied by Cistercian brethren from the abbey of Heiligenkreuz. It is the third-oldest Cistercian abbey in the world with an uninterrupted history.

The abbey church was consecrated in 1159. The architectural elements dating from this time include the Romanesque chapter house with columns and an Early Gothic lavatorium. The Romanesque cloister enclosing a courtyard planted out as a garden, symbolizing paradise, also survives. Other gardens, such as the Terrace and Prelate's gardens, in which exotic plants are still cultivated

today, were added at a later date. The original monastery complex was largely destroyed during the Hussite Wars.

During the 18th century, the abbey, including its church and library, were completely remodeled in the Baroque style and even the church tower, which rises to a height of 269 feet (82 meters), was given a new façade. The abbey continues to support itself from its extensive agricultural, forestry, and fish-farming interests.

Zirc Abbey at Veszprém was founded in 1182 by King Bela III of Hungary, who brought in monks from Clairvaux. It developed into one of Hungary's most important abbeys but was destroyed in 1526 during the Ottoman Wars.

In 1699 it was transferred to the jurisdiction of the Cistercians of Heinrichau, Silesia, who reoccupied it and

Above: the new Baroque church (built 1732–52) of the **Cistercian abbey at Zirc**, an important center of monastic spiritual life in Hungary.

administered it jointly with Heinrichau. It regained its position at the center of monastic life in Hungary by 1712.

Work started on the Baroque abbey church, which boasts magnificent interior furnishings and a famous Egedacher organ, in 1732. The construction of new conventual buildings, including an important natural sciences library where monks systematically researched and described the surrounding Bakony Forest, had already started in 1726. In 1814, Zirc once again became a self-governing abbey, running five grammar schools, but was later united with three other houses. In 1945 a number of its monks fled to the United States (founding a monastery in Dallas, Texas in 1956) and Zirc was dissolved in 1950. Cistercian monks eventually moved back in 1989.

*Left: a view of the Baroque façade of the **church at Stift Zwettl**. The church contains an instrument by the famous organ builder Johann Ignaz Egedacher (1675–1744).*

Premonstratensian abbeys of the Baroque era

The Premonstratensian abbey located in the Wilten district of Innsbruck was built by Bishop Reginbert of Brixen in 1138. According to legend, it was originally founded in around 880 by Haymon, a giant- and dragon-slayer who was converted to Christianity by a monk. A statue of Haymon, standing over 16 feet (5 meters) tall, is still in place in the vestibule of the church.

The original abbey church, an aisled Romanesque pier basilica with choir and a crypt, was rebuilt in the Early Gothic style around 1300. After the collapse of one of the church towers in 1644, Dominikus Löhr (abbot 1651–87) commissioned court architect Christoph Gump (1600–72) to rebuild the church in the Gothic style. The new church was consecrated in 1665 and the north tower completed in 1667. The south tower, however, remained unfinished following Gump's death. The interior was magnificently furnished in the years after 1702 with a high altar and frescoes in the nave and side chapels. The vestibule was given a beautifully crafted wrought-iron grille in 1707.

Strahov Abbey in the Hradčany district of Prague was founded by Vladislav II, duke of Bohemia (reigned 1140–74) in 1140 and colonized by monks from Steinfeld Abbey (Eifel). After being destroyed by a fire in 1258, it was rebuilt but was again badly damaged during the course of various wars in the 15th century.

The Romanesque church of the Assumption, dating from 1148, was expanded after 1258 through the addition of a transept and side chapels in the Gothic style, rebuilt in the Renaissance style in the middle of the 16th century and later completely remodeled in the Baroque style. A heavy bombardment during the Austrian War of Succession in 1740/1 made further work necessary, however. Architect Anselmo Lurago erected the façade towers (1742–58) and divided the ceiling vault into 40 separate fields (stucco cartouches) containing frescoes depicting scenes from the life of the Virgin Mary.

The important monastery library consists of two main rooms. The Theological Room, built between 1661 and 1679 and expanded in 1721, houses the abbey's own collection of manuscripts and books, while the Philosophical Room was built between 1783 and 1790 in order to accommodate the collection of Louka Abbey in Znojmo, Czech Republic.

*Above: the impact of the interior of the **abbey church at Wilten** derives from the contrast between the black varnished woodwork and the white ceiling.*

*Left: the Philosophical Room (designed by Johann Ignaz Palliardi, 1737–1824) of the library at **Strahov Abbey**. The book collection of the Premonstratensian abbey at Louka (Znojmo, Czech Republic) was transferred here in 1784.*

*Opposite page: the **Basilica of Our Lady under the Four Pillars**, located close to the abbey church at Wilten, was rebuilt in the Rococo style between 1751 and 1756. This pilgrim's church has been looked after by Premonstratensian monks from Wilten since 1140.*

Jesuit churches and missions of the Baroque era

The Late Baroque Jesuit church at Mannheim, which is now the seat of the local deanery, was built by the electors Palatine Carl Philipp and Carl Theodor as a court church and dedicated to the Jesuit saints Ignatius of Loyola and Francisco de Xavier (Francis Xavier, 1506–52) in 1760.

In addition to the twin towers of the red sandstone façade, another conspicuous element of this church is its tower-like crossing dome, which rises to a height of 246 feet (75 meters). A number of famous artists contributed to the interior decoration of the church. The marble main altar, which is 66 feet (20 meters) high, and six of the side altars, which are decorated with scenes from the lives of the saints, were created by Peter Anton von Verschaffelt (1710–93), court sculptor from 1752. The celebrated Baroque painter Egid Quirin Asam (1692–1750) was responsible for the frescoes. Asam painted the crossing dome with scenes from the life of Ignatius, the founder of the order, and the ceiling of the nave, with a fresco measuring 4,300 square feet (400 square meters), depicting the journey to the East Indies of missionary Francis Xavier. In April 1750 Asam died in an accident while carrying out this work.

In 1692 the Jesuit missionary Eusebio Francisco Kino (1645–1711) traveled from Mexico to the territory of the Uto-Aztecan Tohono O'odham people at Bac, near present-day Tucson (Arizona, United States). His friendly and sensitive manner helped him to establish 20 missions there. In 1700 he began work on the construction of the San Xavier del Bac mission station, named after the Jesuit missionary Francisco de Xavier who was active in Asia. In 1768 the mission was handed over to the Franciscans, who continue to run it to this day. Between 1783 and 1797, Native Americans under the direction of the mission's padres built a missionary church with side chapels, a famous retable, and wall paintings in the local and Mexican indigenous style. This church is regarded as the most successful example of missionary architecture in the United States. During the 1980s the wall paintings suffered severe water damage and were subsequently restored to their original state by international experts and Native American artists using traditional materials.

*Opposite page: the **Jesuit mission of San Xavier del Bac** near Tucson, US, which is now run by Franciscans and has been nicknamed the "White Dove of the Desert."*

*Right below: the wall paintings of the **mission church of San Xavier del Bac**, including those in the transept shown here, were executed by Native Americans. The interior decoration combines local Native American and Mexican stylistic elements.*

*Right above: the crossing dome and façade with double towers of the **Jesuit church at Mannheim**. Court sculptor Paul Egell (1691–1752) was responsible for the gable reliefs and sculptures of the four cardinal virtues on the façade as well as the famous "Silver Madonna with Corona" inside the church (1747).*

Franciscan monasteries and missions of the Baroque era

The monastery and church of the Annunciation in Ljubljana were built between 1646 and 1660, initially for the Augustinians. In 1784 the complex was taken over by the Franciscans, who continue to maintain it today. The pink façade of this single-nave monastery church with two towers was completed in 1700. Its clear division into two stories and triangular gable terminating in large volutes is reminiscent of Jesuit churches. The gable is crowned by a bronze statue of the Virgin Mary.

In 1738 the interior of the church, containing frescoes and side chapels, was given a large main altar crafted by the sculptor Francesco Robba (1698–1757). The altarpiece by German painter Andreas Herrlein (1738–1817) depicts the *Three Holy Kings*. In the mid-19th century the entire church was decorated by the painter Matevž Langus (1792–1855), but this work was badly damaged in the earthquake of 1895. New ceiling frescoes were painted by the Impressionist Matej Sternen (1870–1949) in 1935/6.

After being made president of the Franciscan mission in California in 1785, Franciscan missionary Fermin Lasuén (1736–1803) founded the Franciscan mission of Santa Barbara in the territory of the Chumash people on the feast day of St. Barbara (4 December) in 1786. This was the first of nine missions founded by Lasuén between 1786 and 1798. It possesses extensive irrigation systems comprising two reservoirs (built in 1806), a dam, a corn mill, and a tannery, as well as pottery kilns.

The original mission chapel was extended on numerous occasions and only acquired its current aspect in 1820 after being rebuilt following a devastating earthquake in December 1812, which destroyed the existing buildings. When Mexico ordered the secularization of the monasteries of southern California in 1833, Santa Barbara became the headquarters of the Franciscan mission in California. It also has a library (California's oldest) housing a collection of over 3,000 manuscripts, which is still run by the Franciscan padres.

*Below: the **Santa Barbara Mission** (California, US). In 1840 the mission became the seat of the Franciscans' own bishop of California and its place of worship raised from the status of chapel to that of pro-cathedral. This entitled it to have two identical towers, a privilege reserved at that time for cathedrals.*

*Right: the entire complex of the **Santa Barbara Mission** showing the mission church and adjoining buildings (drawing based on a wooden model).*

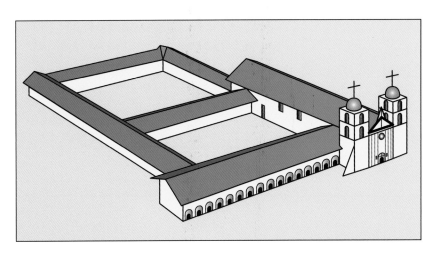

Baroque monastic splendor—the monastery as an integrated work of art

Above all in southern Germany and Austria, the Baroque style has come to predominate in monastic architecture, as nearly all the important abbeys have been remodeled or rebuilt in this style. Baroque monasteries and churches were designed to be harmonious, visually stunning, and integrated works of art (*Gesamtkunstwerk*) and for this reason a special emphasis was placed on the interior decoration of monastery churches based on an infinite variety of images, forms, and lighting effects. The aim was to captivate the beholder—the militant church (Latin: *ecclesia militans*) of the Counter-Reformation had been transformed into the triumphant church (Latin: *ecclesia triumphans*) of the Baroque.

It was no accident that the notion of a vast world stage (Latin: *theatrum mundi*) developed during the Baroque era. Stage effects and optical illusions such as blind vaults, lighting effects, and representations of heaven served to transport congregations from this world to the next.

*The sacristy at **Ettal Abbey**, built in 1714 at the same time as the monastery's library wing, survived the fire of 1744 unscathed. It contains 13 marquetry cabinets (1725–30) for the storage of vestments and altar cloths and hangings.*

Baroque art and architecture also set out to impress through sheer size, through the enormous dimensions of church vaults, altars, and, above all, ceiling frescoes. The altarpieces frequently portray the saints in highly animated scenes. Even Baroque sculptures have lost any hint of the static and seem to speak directly to the viewer through gesture.

During the Late Baroque and Rococo, playfully light stucco work and other decorative elements came to the fore, often endowing monastery churches with an overpowering wealth of detail. Another conspicuous feature is the play of light, based on the use of highly effective light/dark contrasts, and the use of different color schemes for different themes. Gold, white, and azure, for example, were the preferred colors for depictions of the church triumphant. The wooden superstructure of altars and pulpits adopted supple forms and warm and solid hues. In terms of theme, the paintings and frescoes adorning Baroque monastery rooms and libraries often combined Christian subjects with classical mythology.

*Above: the High Baroque and Rococo altars in the **abbey church at Ettal**. The side altars and pulpit were created by the leading Rococo sculptor Johann Baptist Straub (1704–84) between 1757 and 1765.*

*Left: the interior of the **church of Weltenburg Abbey** was designed by the brothers Cosmas Damian and Egid Quirin Asam, who created a Gesamtkunstwerk with their unification of spatial architecture, dramatic lighting, painting, and sculpture.*

Nineteenth-century Monasteries

During the 19th century the monastic orders and their architecture adopted forms that breathed new life into the ideals of earlier times. Against this background there was a surge of interest in the strict Trappist order. In 1794, monks who had fled from the dissolved mother house of La Trappe, in France, founded a monastic community on a farm at Westmalle, Belgium, which was elevated to the status of abbey (Our Lady of the Sacred Heart) in 1836. Between 1830 and 1900, monastic buildings in the neo-Romanesque style were erected and the abbey earned a reputation for its produce—most importantly beer and cheese. In 1860, Trappists from Alsace acquired the dilapidated buildings of a pilgrimage church in Mariawald in the Eifel, which had previously been serviced by Cistercians, and over the following 30 years built a new complex that was raised to the status of abbey in 1909. Despite periods of temporary suppression—during the Prussian *Kulturkampf* (power struggle between Church and State, 1875–87) and by the Gestapo on a charge of "activities hostile to the state" in 1941, when the abbey was used as a field hospital—Mariawald is still in existence today, Trappist monks having moved back in 1945.

The monastic buildings and church of Mariawald Abbey in the Eifel, Germany's only Trappist monastery.

The Trappist order and the vow of silence

The Carthusians having already demonstrated their fascination with the strictest of monastic rules, Armand-Jean Le Bouthilier de Rancé (1626–1700), abbot of the French Cistercian monastery of La Trappe, propagated a form of monastic life based on self-denial, humility, and radical asceticism in 1657. The Trappist reform movement, also known as the "Cistercians of the Strict Observance," adopted strict rules of silence, abstinence, and acts of penance that originally included physical self-castigation.

Trappist monks pray in the abbey church seven times a day and spend the rest of their time in strict seclusion and silence, which is why they (like the Carthusians) discharge no pastoral duties outside the monastery. Their rule prescribes heavy manual labor (particularly in agriculture and cultivation of the land, as Trappist monks are expected to earn their own keep) as a counterweight to their life of contemplation, penance, and prayer. In contrast to the now small Carthusian community, the Trappists currently have 100 male and 67 female houses.

A Trappist monk reading in the library of the Abbey of Our Lady of Gethsemane in Louisville, Kentucky, US.

Left: the South Vat at **Westmalle Abbey**, *where 32,000 gallons (120,000 liters) of the famous Trappist beer are brewed each year with which the monastery has financed itself since 1856. In 1934 the first "triple" beer (a dark, strong beer with a high alcohol content) was produced here.*

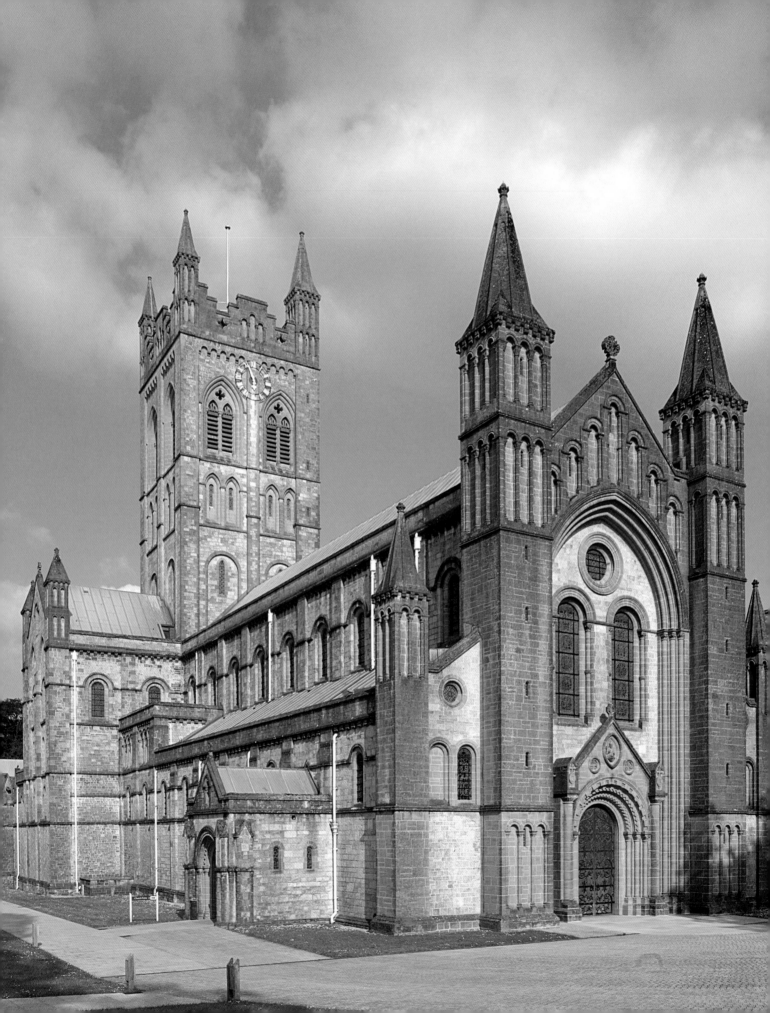

During the 19th century the Benedictine and Trappist orders experienced a growth in numbers, particularly in the largely Protestant United Kingdom and United States. Many of their abbeys were built in the neo-Romanesque or neo-Gothic styles, making a deliberate architectural reference to the great age of the monastery in medieval Europe.

In 1854, a group of Benedictine monks from Einsiedeln Abbey in Switzerland founded the monastic community of St. Meinrad in Spencer County, Indiana, US. Elevated to abbey status in 1870, and made one of only 11 archabbeys in the world in 1954, the community had established a philosophical-theological university as early as 1861, a publishing house in 1867, and a mission academy in 1878. Work began on the abbey church in 1858. In 1887 the entire complex burned down but was rebuilt within the space of three years. Today, some 105 monks live at St. Meinrad Archabbey, whose enormous estates and monastery businesses employ around 500 people.

In 1846, Benedictines from Metten in Bavaria founded the abbey of St. Vincent in Latrobe, Pennsylvania, US. This was the first Benedictine abbey in the US and was also soon elevated to archabbey status. Under the guidance of the German monk Bonifaz Wimmer (abbot 1846–87), St. Vincent Archabbey soon founded numerous daughter houses, including St. Mary's Priory in Newark, New Jersey, US in 1857, which was originally serviced by German immigrants. St. Mary's became independent in 1884 and in 1968 was renamed St. Mary's in Newark Abbey.

Buckfast Abbey in England (Devon) was founded as a Benedictine Abbey in 1018, but moved to the Cistercians in 1147 and was dissolved in 1539. In 1882, monks who had been driven out of France during the power struggle between Church and State, bought the monastery ruins and founded a new Benedictine community there, which was raised to the status of abbey in 1902. The abbey church was constructed between 1907 and 1937 and given modern windows and a new floor in 1968. The abbey finances itself through agriculture and large-scale beekeeping and runs its own education center.

*Above: in 2007, monks and students celebrated the 150th anniversary of the **Benedictine abbey of St. Mary's in Newark** (New Jersey, US) in the choir of the abbey church.*

*Left: architecturally, the church of the **Benedictine archabbey of St. Meinrad in Indiana** harks back to the Middle Ages. St. Meinrad is one of two archabbeys in the US.*

*Opposite page: the **church of Buckfast Abbey** was completed in 1937 in the Norman and Early Gothic styles. This Benedictine foundation is one of the few monasteries in the United Kingdom that remain active today.*

Twentieth-century Monasteries

The monastic buildings of the 20th century display the whole range of architectural styles from updated versions of traditional building types to avant-garde and experimental approaches. For the buildings of Mepkin Abbey, a Trappist house founded in 1949 on the site of a historic plantation in Charleston, a restrained modern style was chosen. The abbey is famous for its library and gardens, originally laid out in 1936 and redesigned in 1988.

In 1953 the Dominican order commissioned one of the most important architects of the century, Le Corbusier (1887–1965), to redesign its priory and college of Sainte Marie de la Tourette, in Évreux, France. The result, built between 1956 and 1961, was a reinforced concrete frame structure (dedicated in 1960) with four wings and fixed glazing (ventilation is by means of air slits with shutters) on a sloping site. Facing uphill the building has three stories and, facing downhill, five. On the upward-facing side the building rests on free-standing pillars. Inside, there are five floor levels, each of whose rooms are of varying heights.

The architectural influence of both Le Corbusier and La Tourette can be seen clearly in the abbey of Las Condes near Santiago de Chile. This Benedictine community was founded by English monks in 1938. It became a priory in 1959 and was raised to the status of abbey in 1980. Between 1949 and 1975 it was part of the Benedictine congregation of Beuron, which devotes itself primarily to liturgy. The

*The **Dominican college of Sainte Marie de la Tourette in Évreux**. Prior to starting work, Le Corbusier explored in depth the problem of how to express a sense of spirituality through architecture.*

*Left: the white concrete **abbey church at Las Condes near Santiago de Chile**, with its square bell tower, is modeled on La Tourette, the Dominican monastic center designed by Le Corbusier.*

*Below: a procession of monks outside **Mepkin Abbey in Charleston** (South Carolina, US). In 1949 the owners of the estate welcomed the arrival of 29 Trappist monks.*

abbey's new church, designed by Chilean architects Gabriel Guarda and Martin Correa, was built between 1961 and 1964. It is a concrete structure in the strict geometric and rectangular style of La Tourette.

The entrance level, comprising doorway, day room and library, is on the third story (Level 3). The story below (Level 4) accommodates the chapter house and refectory while below that (Level 5) are the cellars. The monks' cells are on the upper stories (Levels 1 and 2; 50 living cells on each floor). The inner courtyard has a cruciform cloister and leads into the plain, rectangular, single-story church of cast concrete, which has light slits and a projecting crypt.

The monasteries and religious orders by no means remained aloof from the events of the 20th century. As had previously happened at Plötzensee Prison in Berlin (a place of execution under the Third Reich) and at the concentration

camp at Dachau, in 1984 a community of 14 Carmelite nuns set up an expiatory convent at Auschwitz extermination camp in the Theater Building next to the electric fence and Extermination Block 11. Sustained international protests by Jewish organizations fearful of a "Christian occupation" of this place of unutterable cruelty led the Carmelites to move out in 1993 and take up residence in a building in the neighboring town of Oświecim, Poland.

In 1999, seven Trappist nuns from Iowa, US established a monastic community on the western edge of the Norwegian island of Tautra, not far from a Cistercian abbey that had been founded in 1207 and dissolved in 1537. A modern abbey church designed by the architect Jan Olav (born 1959) was completed in 2006. The Mariakloster finances itself by manufacturing fine herbal soaps and with a small publishing venture.

In 1928 a group of Benedictine monks from the abbey of St. Ottilien in Bavaria took over a public school in Meschede and founded a community there. In 1932 Königsmünster became a priory and in 1956 (after having been dissolved between 1941 and 1945) was elevated to the status of self-governing abbey. In 1960 the architect Hans Schilling (1921–2009) presented his plans for a modern abbey church. The Friedenskirche (Peace Church) was built between 1962 and 1964 and in the organization of its interior reflects the liturgical reforms recommended by the Second Vatican Council. Under Stephan Schröer (abbot 1976–2001), the abbey developed into a community of 80 Benedictine monks, although this figure had fallen to 59 by 2007. The abbey's architecture, including the church and the "House of Contemplation" designed by the architect Peter Kulka (born in 1937) has been widely acclaimed. The monks work in education and provide pastoral care to the local parish. A number are also actively involved in missionary work in Korea and Africa.

*Above: the **Carmelite expiatory convent** established in a former SS building opposite the extermination block at Auschwitz, where the canonized martyr Father Maximilian Kolbe was murdered in 1941. The convent was moved to another site in 1993.*

*Left: the **church of Tautra Mariakloster**, whose wooden trusses give it a light, floating quality.*

*Opposite page: the **"Peace Church"** of the Benedictine abbey of **Königsmünster** in **Meschede**, Germany, still looks extremely modern even 40 years after it was built.*

*Left: the façade of **Tautra Mariakloster** in Norway, whose modern design featuring abundant windows and walls of glass allows for a bright, open interior.*

The Monasteries of Eastern Christendom

Monasteries of the Greek Orthodox Church

Like the monasteries of western Christendom, the monastic life of the Orthodox churches also combines contemplation with active love of one's neighbor and pastoral care. The monastic father St. Basil the Great (c. 330–79) to whom the Greek Orthodox Church owes most of its monastic rules, recommended a communal life based on humility, patience, and consideration.

Monasticism's roots in the secluded lives of religious hermits is all the more apparent in the case of the most ancient Orthodox monasteries. In 478 St. Sabbas (c. 439–532) withdrew to a cavern outside Jerusalem. In 483, having been imitated by others, he founded the monastery that bears his name, Mar Saba (Palestine's oldest monastery), on the cliffside of Kidron Valley southwest of Jerusalem. In 501, seven years after becoming archimandrite (superior) of all monastic settlements in the Jerusalem region, he began work on the construction of the main church (*katholikon*) of his monastery, where he was later buried. In the Middle Ages his relics were stolen by western crusaders and brought to Venice; they were eventually returned to Mar Saba in a solemn ceremony in 1964, during the papacy of Pope Paul VI.

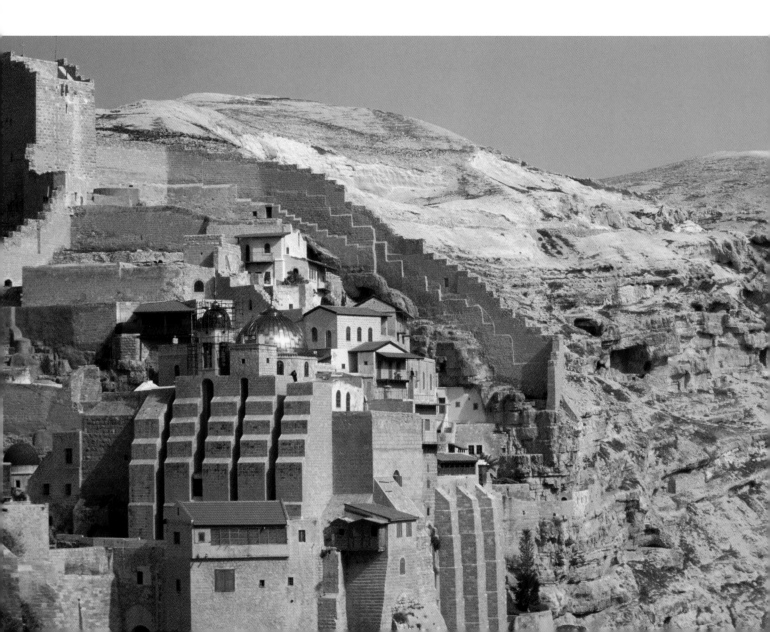

Despite being destroyed by the Persians in 614 and the Arabs in 636, some 4,000–5,000 monks lived in the labyrinthine monastic complex of Mar Saba and in the surrounding caves during the 7th century. In 1840 the Russian czar, Nicholas I (reigned 1826–55), had the monastery restored. Around the turn of the 20th century there were still 50 monks living at the monastery; today there are just 10. In 1958 a letter written by the church father St. Clement of Alexandria (c. 150–215) was discovered at Mar Saba containing a fragment of the Secret Gospel of St. Mark, an alternative version of the first Christian gospel.

Between 450 and 463, the Byzantine consul Stoudios built a monastery with an aisled basilica in Constantinople. It was dedicated to St. John the Baptist but became known by the name of its founder. This was the monastery of the famous monk Theodore the Studdite (759–826), whose ascetic monastic rule was to have a decisive influence on monastic life in Byzantium and Russia. In the 8th and 9th centuries over 700 monks lived at Stoudios Monastery. It was badly damaged during the Crusades and in 1486 was transformed into the mosque of Imrahor Camii. It was eventually destroyed in an earthquake in the 19th century.

*Left: a monk opening a door at **Mar Saba Monastery outside Jerusalem**. To this day, women are still denied access to the monastery buildings.*

*Opposite page: shown here clinging to the cliffside are the buildings of **Mar Saba Monastery, Jerusalem**. From 712 until his death, St. John of Damascus (c. 650–before 754), regarded as the last of the church fathers, lived and wrote here.*

*Left: the ruins of the **church of Stoudios Monastery in Istanbul** (Constantinople), an aisled, galleried basilica with narthex, polygonal apse, and a marble floor dating from the 11th century.*

The complex of St. Catherine's Monastery, surrounded by defensive walls. The monastery was built in the early Byzantine style at the foot of Mount Sinai (Gebel Musa) in Egypt.

St. Catherine's Monastery on Mount Sinai

St. Catherine's Monastery on Mount Sinai is one of the oldest monasteries in Christendom. It was built at an altitude of 5,000 feet (1,500 meters) in a barren landscape on the spot where God spoke to Moses from the burning bush. During her pilgrimage to the Holy Land, Helena, the mother of Emperor Constantine, erected a chapel here in 324 around which the Byzantine emperor Justinian I (reigned 527–65) built the present monastery between 548 and 565.

The monastery church was also constructed at this time and the entire complex (249 x 279 feet/76 x 85 meters) enclosed by a defensive wall for the protection of the monks. The significance of the monastery is partly due to

the fact that, although some of the monastic buildings were destroyed by an earthquake in 1312 (and subsequently rebuilt by 1461), it has never in its entire history been attacked or plundered. According to the Muslim tradition, Muhammad was a guest at the monastery a number of times before his receiving his calling from God, and is supposed to have urged his followers to place St. Catherine's under his protection rather than attacking it. In around 1000 a mosque was erected within the monastery precincts immediately next to the basilica, in order, it is thought, to protect the complex from anti-Christian measures being taken by the fanatical Fatimid caliph al-Hakim (reigned 996–1021). In 1099 the Crusaders placed the monastery under their protection during their conquest of Jerusalem.

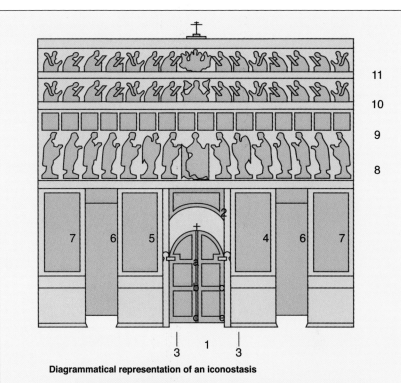

Diagrammatical representation of an iconostasis

1   Central doors: Holy Doors, Royal Doors with depictions of the Annunciation (a) and the evangelists (b–e)

2   Picture of the Last Supper

3   Columns

4   Icon depicting Christ or the patron saint of the church

5   Picture of the Mother of God

6   North and south doors with pictures of the archangels or saintly deacons

7   Icons of various kinds

8   Frieze with Deesis (depiction of Christ in Majesty on the Day of Judgment)

9   Frieze with 12–16 smaller icons depicting the main feasts of the ecclesiastical year

10 Depiction of the prophets on either side of the Virgin Mary

11 Depiction of the patriarchs and other Old Testament figures on either side of the Trinity

It is said that a monk had a vision in which angels transported the body of the revered martyr St. Catherine (of Alexandria) to Mount Sinai, where it was discovered by monks in around 800. Her relics (skull and left hand) are still venerated in the monastery church today.

Thanks to the protection of the Muslims, the monastery was spared during the Byzantine Iconoclasm (726–842, see p. 121). The monastery's collection of over 2,000 icons, many of which can be seen in the narthex of the church, therefore includes some of the oldest surviving examples in the world. In the 17th century the monastery came under the control of the autonomous monastic republic of Mount Athos and continues to enjoy the same self-governing status today.

Above: iconostases (the one depicted here is Russian) are walls of icons containing three doors. In Orthodox churches they divide the nave (and therefore the congregation) from the sanctuary (see also p. 120).

Left: heaped against one of the whitewashed walls in the ossuary of St. Catherine's Monastery are the skulls of deceased monks. Behind them sits another pile containing their bones.

Because St. Catherine's Monastery was never plundered, its library is of inestimable value to the study of early Christianity. There are 4 rooms containing 6,000 manuscripts in their original bindings and in every known language spoken in the early Christian world; 3,000 of them date from antiquity and some are older than the monastery itself.

It was here that the German theologian Konstantin von Tischendorf (1815–74) discovered the 4th-century Codex Sinaiticus—the oldest-known, near-complete manuscript of the Bible, copied out onto 346.5 folios (sheets)—between 1844 and 1859. The story of how the greater part of this manuscript ended up in museums in St. Petersburg, London, and Leipzig is the stuff of crime fiction of a highly unusual, academic kind and, as the monks have been demanding their return for decades, remains the subject of controversy today. Since the 1990s, researchers from various countries have been studying the collection of the monastery with renewed interest, but the monks have become more cautious and never allow any of their texts to leave the monastery.

*Opposite page: the interior of the monastery church, the "**Church of the Transfiguration," of St. Catherine's Monastery on Mount Sinai**. Its bell tower contains nine bells including an ancient wooden one.*

This icon of the Virgin Mary from the monastery of Agiou Pavlou in the monastic republic of Mount Athos shows the Mother of God with the Infant Jesus.

Icons and the Byzantine Iconoclasm

Icons (from the Greek *eikón*, meaning image) are the religious symbols of the Orthodox churches. They developed out of images of Christ, the Virgin Mary, and the saints, which were believed to be capable of working miracles and enjoyed a special, revered status within the context of Orthodox liturgy and worship.

The veneration of images was always a controversial issue in Christianity. While those who venerated images (the iconodules) saw them as a reflection of the divine process whereby Jesus assumed a visible, human form, those opposed to religious images (the iconoclasts) based their arguments on the Old Testament prohibition of the worship of idols. In 726 in Byzantium, Emperor Leo III (reigned 717–41) unleashed a campaign of destruction of images, known as the "Byzantine Iconoclasm." It unfolded in a number of different phases up to 842 and brought the empire to the brink of collapse.

As staunch venerators of images, monasteries and monks resisted the campaign fiercely, and the ensuing struggle led to the destruction of monasteries, civil war, and assassinations. In 842 the council in Constantinople finally decreed that the veneration of images be permitted.

Above: resting on the metal shelves of the four rooms comprising the library of St. Catherine's Monastery are numerous bibliographical treasures of Christianity. The monastery library is regarded as the most important repository of Christian writings after the Vatican.

*The **monastery of St. John** on the island of Patmos towers fortress-like above the town. Patmos is believed to be the place where St. John the Evangelist wrote his Revelation, the last book of the New Testament.*

Monasteries in Greece

The monastery of Panagia Chozoviotissa, which clings to the steep slopes of Mount Profitis Ilias on the island of Amorgos in the Cyclades, was founded in the 9th century by monks from Palestine. It was built overlooking the bay from which a miraculous icon of the Virgin Mary was washed ashore. Still venerated in the monastery church today, the image is supposed to have been thrown into the sea during the Byzantine Iconoclasm by a devout woman who wanted to save it from destruction. After being sacked by pirates, the monastery was rebuilt by Emperor Alexius I Comnenus (reigned 1081–1118) and houses a number of famous manuscripts from the 11th to the 13th centuries, as well as a school. Until its expropriation in 1952 it was the wealthiest monastery in Greece.

The monastery of Hosios Loukas near Delphi was built on the site where the hermit St. Lukas had founded his monastic community in 946. After his death in 953, the burial place of this monk venerated for his prophetic gifts became both a destination for pilgrims and a monastery,

with a refectory (now a museum) and monks' cells grouped around two churches.

The Panagia church, the smaller of the two (built 959–63) connects with the larger church of St. Loukas completed in 1011, a domed cross-in-square church of simple brick construction. The main church, dome, and crypt, containing the sarcophagus of St. Lukas, are decorated with 11th-century mosaics.

The "holy" island of Patmos is thought to be the place of exile of St. John the Evangelist and the location of the cave in which he wrote his Book of Revelation. In 1088 the blessed monk Christodoulos founded the monastery of St. John on the island. Protected by strong defensive walls, the complex has been extended several times over the centuries. In the 12th century the church was given a marble floor with inset mosaics as well as frescoes and murals. Located below the church are the monks' cells and the monastery's famous library containing over 900 manuscripts and 15,000 ancient books. The complex has two chapels: a chapel of the Virgin Mary and the funerary chapel of Christodoulos containing the saint's sarcophagus of wood and silver.

Above left: due to its location, **Panagia Chozoviotissa***, which clings to a cliffside on the island of Amorgos, is regarded as one of Greece's most attractive monasteries.*

Above right: the crypt at the **monastery of Hosios Loukas** *with its painted ceiling vault resting on pillars. This is the place where the relics of the prophetic monk St. Lukas are venerated.*

Left: general view of the **monastery of Hosios Loukas near Delphi***. The entire complex consists of the monks' wing and two monastery churches with bell tower.*

The name of Daphni Monastery outside Athens means "laurel"—the plant of the god Apollo—and is thought to refer to a shrine to Apollo here, on the site of which an early monastery and church, enclosed by defensive walls, were built in the 5th century. The ruins of this original complex, which was abandoned in the 7th century, can still be seen.

The present-day monastery with its domed cross-in-square church of simple brick construction was built in 1080 and decorated with fine mosaics, among which the dome mosaic of Christus Pantokrator stands out in particular. In 1206 the monastery was conquered by Roman Catholic crusaders and given to Cistercian monks from Bellevaux Abbey in France, who remodeled the complex along western lines. In 1458 the Ottomans returned the monastery to Orthodox monks. In 1821, having become a center of the Greek struggle for independence, Daphni Monastery was burned down by the Turks and had to be abandoned by its monks. A comprehensive program of restoration was launched in 1889 which paid special attention to the mosaics.

Nea Moni (New Monastery), dedicated to the Assumption of the Virgin Mary and located in a cypress grove on the island of Chios, was founded in 1042 by Emperor Constantine IX Monomachos (reigned 1042–55) on the site where three monks had found an icon of the Virgin Mary in a myrrh bush. Constantine had pledged to endow a monastery if he ever became emperor and this he duly did by marrying Zoe (reigned 1042), the daughter of the reigning emperor.

The monastery complex consists of the main church, two smaller churches, a refectory, and the monks' wing. This richly appointed monastery has famous mosaics depicting scenes from the life of Christ, a Pantokrator mosaic in the dome and images of the Virgin Mary, the archangels, and various saints. As a place of refuge for local citizens caught up in the Greek War of Independence, the monastery was burned down by the Turks during the Chios Massacre of 1822 and the library sacked. This action led to the deaths of 600 monks. Nea Moni was restored several times from 1857 onwards, a job which was made difficult by the collapse of the dome and bell tower in an earthquake in 1881.

*Below: the narthex (vestibule) of the **monastery church of Nea Moni on the island of Chios** is decorated with mosaics. This view looking south shows a mosaic depicting Christ praying in the Garden of Gethsemane and the betrayal of Judas.*

Below: this mosaic of the Resurrection in the katholikon *(main church) of **Daphni Monastery** is one of a cycle depicting the life and suffering of Christ.*

*Right: **Daphni Monastery outside Athens** showing the mountains in the background. The monastery church, famed for its mosaics, is dedicated to the Dormition of the Virgin.*

Monasteries on Crete

Moni Kardiotissa, also known as Panagia Kera, was built at the beginning of the 14th century. What was initially a single-room chapel was later expanded into a double-nave monastery church with brick windows and blind arcades. In 1970 a series of frescoes dating from the time of the monastery's foundation was discovered beneath the whitewashed walls, including one of the Ascension of Christ. The main icon venerated here (of the Virgin Mary) was stolen twice by the Turks and is said to have been returned to the monastery in a miraculous way each time. After being stolen for a third time it was chained to a column in Istanbul before reappearing at Moni Kardiotissa together with the column.

According to legend, Arkadi Monastery was founded by Emperor Flavius Arcadius (reigned 395–408) but it is probably more recent than that. In 1587 the Venetians, then lords of Crete, started work on the construction of the current double-nave structure to replace the previous building, whose ruins can still be seen on the northwest side of the complex. Particularly impressive is the façade of the new church in a combination of Cretan and Venetian styles.

Arkadi Monastery was destroyed in 1669 during the Turkish occupation of Crete, and subsequently rebuilt. In 1866 it became a center of Crete resistance to the Ottomans. While under siege by Turkish troops, some 1,000 revolutionaries and monks deliberately blew themselves up by igniting the monastery's gunpowder store. Another monastery that played a leading role in Crete's wars of liberation, above all through the establishment of so-called secret schools, which the monks used as a way of leading the Christian resistance, was Preveli. The original buildings are thought to have been built in the 10th or 11th century. The present complex consists of two separate monasteries: a smaller one dedicated to John the Baptist, and a larger one dedicated to St. John the Evangelist. Its double-nave hall church was consecrated in 1836 but possesses a belfry dating from 1629. A cruciform reliquary cross containing a fragment of Christ's cross is venerated here and is held to have miraculous powers. The complex has been destroyed in battle on numerous occasions, but has been lavishly restored each time.

*Above: the small **monastery chapel at Moni Kardiotissa** was enlarged in the 14th century.*

*Right: **Arkadi Monastery**, built of rough-hewn stone, resembles a fortress and served this purpose during the mass suicide that took place here in 1866, an event that stunned the whole of Europe. The monastery is now served by just a handful of monks.*

*Opposite page: view of the interior of the main **church of Preveli Monastery**, dedicated to St. John the Evangelist, showing its famous wooden iconostasis (dividing wall between nave and sanctuary).*

The monasteries of Metéora

*A view of the **monastery of Metamórphosis**, also known as Megálo Metéoro, the largest and highest of the Metéora monasteries.*

The monasteries of Metéora (Greek *meteorizo*: suspended in the air) sit atop the summits of rock pillars at the foot of the Pindus Mountains in Thessaly and give the impression of indeed hovering between heaven and earth. Some of them are almost inaccessible and until the 1920s could only be reached by means of nets or panniers raised and lowered by hoists.

As long ago as the 11th century, small hermitages were established here. They gradually amalgamated to form the monastery of Doúpiani, which no longer exists but is commemorated by a small chapel. It was not until 1334, however, with the arrival of 16 monks from Mount Athos, that the monastic community started to thrive. Their leader St. Athanasius (c. 1302–80) founded the monastery of Metamórphosis in 1344 and composed a monastic rule for the monasteries of Metéora. Athanasius is still venerated today as the founding father of the Meteorites. From the 13th century onwards, rulers and wealthy private individuals endowed further monasteries, often with rich furnishings, until eventually there were 24 independent monasteries and hermitages here.

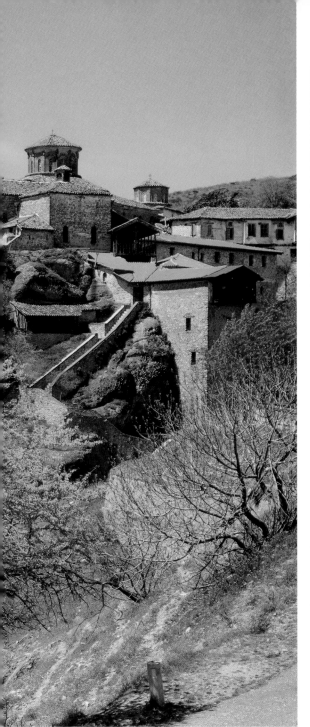

Most of them no longer remain. Some fell into decay and were abandoned in the 19th century, while others were destroyed, such as—in the 19th century—Agios Dimitrios, a place of refuge for Greek revolutionaries, and Agios Nikólaos Bádovas by German occupation forces in 1943.

Six of the monasteries are still inhabited today and are open to visitors. There are four men's (Metamórphosis, Agios Nikólaos Anapavsás, Agia Triáda, and Varlaám) and two women's convents (Rousánou and Agios Stéphanos). Metamórphosis, also known as "Great Metéoron" (Mégalo Metéoro), is the largest of the six, occupying a site (including monastery buildings and gardens) of nearly 15 acres (60,000 square meters). At an altitude of over 2,000 feet (613 meters), it is also the highest. The name Metéoro ("suspended in the air") was conferred on it by Athanasius, whose hermit's cave is located by the monastery entrance. Construction started in the middle of the 14th century and was completed in 1388. The dome of the cruciform church, which is dedicated to the Resurrection of Christ, is adorned with a depiction of Christus Pantokrator, while frescoes dating from 1483 and 1552 grace the walls. The summit has been made accessible via a tunnel containing 143 steps.

*Above: a fresco in the **Metéora monastery of Rousánou**, which has been inhabited by nuns since the 1950s.*

*Below: the **Metéora monastery of Agia Triáda**, which until 1925 was only accessible with the help of winches and rope ladders.*

Agios Nikólaos Anapavsás is famed above all for its monastery church dedicated to John the Baptist. In 1527 it was decorated with frescoes and murals by Theophanes Streletzás Bathas (c. 1500–59), the most important exponent of the Cretan school of church painting, who later worked in the monasteries of Mount Athos. Here too the skulls of deceased monks were stored on shelves.

Agia Triáda, dedicated to the Holy Trinity, only became accessible by foot (thanks to the construction of steps) in 1925. Thought to have been built between 1458 and 1476, the monastery has frescoes dating from 1741 and houses a printed Book of the Gospels of 1539 that originated in Venice.

The monastery of Varlaám was built between 1518 and 1538 on the site of an abandoned 14th-century hermitage and possesses two monastery churches. Like those of most of the monasteries of Metéora, the monks of Varlaám live under cenobitic conditions: in a confined community, under uniform leadership, and with no personal possessions.

Rousánou, founded in 1388, was (like Arsánou) reinvigorated by the hermits Joasaph and Maximos in 1525, but fell into decline after being attacked and plundered several times and was eventually abandoned in 1940. The monastery's treasures were given to the monastery of

Metamórphosis. Since the 1950s it has been put to new use as a women's convent. Its church is decorated with 16th-century frescoes.

Agios Stéphanos was built in the 14th century on the site of a hermitage dating from 1192. Tradition has it that Emperor Andronicus III Paleologus (reigned 1328–41) was entertained so hospitably here that he showered the monastery with gifts, earning it the epithet "Royal." In the 19th century there were still 30 monks living here, but their number fell steadily and in 1961 it was turned—like Rousánou—into a women's convent.

Opposite page above: the Metéora monastery of Agios Stéphanos, which is famous for its gardens. The nuns who currently inhabit the monastery run a school for orphaned girls.

Opposite page below: the Metéora monastery of Varlaám possesses two churches decorated with frescoes and abundant icons.

Above: a niche containing an icon of St. Barbara in the church of Rousánou convent for women.

Right: the Metéora monastery of Rousánou, which is only accessible via a bridge from the neighboring cliff, was probably built over the remains of an older church.

The monasteries of Mount Athos

The best known of Orthodox monastic communities is the autonomous monastic republic of Mount Athos, which occupies a promontory of the Greek peninsula of Chalcidice measuring barely 130 square miles (336 square kilometers). Mount Athos was inhabited by hermits living according to early Christian monastic ideals long before the monk Athanasius the Athonite (c. 925–1000) founded the monastery under a common rule, Great Lavra, in 963.

During the course of the centuries, 20 major monasteries were built on Athos (17 Greek Orthodox, 1 Russian Orthodox, 1 Bulgarian Orthodox, and 1 Serbian Orthodox), each of which is self-governing and elects its own abbot. In addition to the large monasteries, there are also 12 monks' settlements known as *sketae*, huts (*kalvia*) shared by several monks, cells (*kellia*) for individual monks, plus a number of hermitages. Hermits also continue to live on the slopes of Mount Athos in caves or shacks, recalling the beginnings of monastic life on the promontory. The monasteries were all built to the same basic plan: a square fortress with defensive walls and watchtowers to guard against frequent raids by pirates. The capital and administrative seat of the monastic republic is Karyés, which has its own amenities including post office, bank, and police station, as well as being the location of the Agios Andrea *skete* and the largest Orthodox church in the whole of the Balkans. A parliament comprising two monks from each of the major monasteries also meets here. Access to the monastic republic of Mount Athos is prohibited for all females including female animals. There are currently 2,262 monastics living in the republic, whereas in 1903 there were 7,432 monks in the 20 large monasteries alone.

Ever since the 16th century, there has been a fixed hierarchy of the major monasteries. The highest and most venerable is the founding monastery, Great Lavra (Moni Megistis Lavra), built in 963. With its large church, defensive walls and 15 towers (not all of which survive), it became a model for many other Orthodox monasteries. The founder, Athanasius, who moved here with around 80 monks and is buried in a monastery chapel, died when the dome of the church collapsed. Great Lavra's famous library contains over 2,000 manuscripts, 800 of which date from the Byzantine era.

*The fortress-like **Stavronikita** (see p. 134) ranks fifteenth in the hierarchy of Athonite monasteries and is also the smallest.*

*Right: the chapel within the inner precincts of the **Mount Athos monastery of Megistis Lavra** (Great Lavra). In 964 the maximum number of monks permitted to live here was set at 80.*

*Right below: magnificent wall paintings from the 15th century adorn the corridors and church of **Megistis Lavra**, the oldest of the Mount Athos monasteries.*

*Above: in keeping with Orthodox monastic tradition, the skulls of deceased monks are stored on wooden shelves and grouped around a small altar in the ossuary of **Agiou Panteleimonas**.*

In 964, just one year after it was founded, Emperor Nicephoras II Phocas (reigned 963–969) decreed that Great Lavra should be independent from the Church authorities and became a model copied by all the other Athos monasteries. In 1535 the monastery rooms and church were decorated by the famous monk and painter Theophanes Streletzás Bathas, who had previously worked in the monasteries of Metéora.

Moni Stavronikita, the smallest of the monasteries and the latest to be officially consecrated (1536), was first mentioned in 1020 and is thought to have been built in the 10th century by the hermits Stavros and Nikitas. After falling into decline it was acquired by the monk Gregorios Girameriatis in 1533 and rebuilt with the support of Jeremias I, patriarch of Constantinople 1522–46, who is commemorated as founder in a wall painting in the monastery. The monastery church contains an important mosaic icon of St. Nicholas dating from the 14th century and wall paintings by Theophanes Streletzás Bathas. Gutted by fire 5 times over the centuries, the monastery accommodates 40 monks today.

Moni Xenofondos, dedicated to St. George, was founded in 998 by the monk Xenophon, after whom it is named, and from the 11th century onward grew powerful thanks to the patronage of the Byzantine imperial court. The monastery has two churches. The older church dates from the 16th century and contains a cycle of frescoes by the Cretan painter Antonios, while the more recent one was built between 1817 and 1837 following a devastating fire and is the largest Greek Orthodox monastery church on Mount Athos.

Moni Agiou Panteleimonas, also known as Rossikon (the Russian monastery), dates from the 9th century. It first came into the hands of Russian brethren in 1163, only to be abandoned by them in 1735. Rebuilt from 1765 onwards, initially by Greek monks, it was taken over once more by Russian monks in 1840. Thanks to the patronage of the Russian czars, it subsequently became the largest monastery on Athos in terms of numbers. In 1913 there were 2,000 monks living here; now there are just 50. In addition to an important library, the monastery of St. Pantaleon possesses an icon (forming part of its gold-leaf-covered iconostasis) and the skull of its patron saint.

*Left: general view of the **Mount Athos monastery of Xenofondos**. Its crenellated tower lends the complex, in which 35 monks now live, a military appearance.*

*Opposite page: the colorful church domes and bell tower of the **Mount Athos monastery of Agiou Panteleimonas**.*

Orthodox monasteries in Bulgaria

One of the largest of all Orthodox monasteries, Rila Monastery was founded in a valley of the Rila Mountains by the monk St. John of Rila (876–946), Bulgaria's first hermit and patron saint. Through numerous endowments, the Bulgarian czars made it an important center of Bulgarian spiritual and cultural life. After being plundered and destroyed by the Ottomans in the middle of the 15th century, it was quickly rebuilt. Of the old buildings, only the defensive tower of the Chreljes church of 1334 survives, adjacent to which a bell tower was erected in 1844.

*The inner courtyard of **Rila Monastery**, enclosed by the monks' wings with their arcaded walkways. In the center is the monastery church.*

As a center of national identity, the entire complex was rebuilt from 1816 onwards by some 3,000 craftsmen, who (despite a devastating fire in 1833) gave the monastery its current form. The main church of Sweta Bogorodica (Holy Mother of God), built between 1834 and 1837, with five domes, a gallery, and three altar niches, is decorated with a series of frescoes that were completed in 1846. The four-story monastery buildings contain 300 monks' cells. The monastery possesses valuable icons and manuscripts as well as the extremely intricate "Rafail's Cross," a carved crucifix incorporating 650 minute figures in 104 religious scenes measuring just 32 x 17 inches (81 x 43 centimeters).

Bulgaria's second-largest monastery, located southwest of Plovdiv, is Bachkovo Monastery, founded in 1083 by the Byzantine army commander Grigori Bakuriani (originally from Georgia) and his brother Abasi (the Bulgarian word *bachko* means brother). Bakuriani's funerary chapel, dating from the time of the monastery's foundation, still survives. The monastery, famed for its religious school, was initially colonized by Georgian monks until being turned into a center of Bulgarian spiritual life by the Bulgarian czar Ivan Alexander (reigned 1331–71).

Bachkovo was also destroyed by the Ottomans in the middle of the 15th century; its monastic buildings were rebuilt by 1601, and the main monastery church of Sweta Bogorodica by 1604. The church contains a reputedly miracle-working icon of a three-handed Mother of God (Virgin Mary Eleusa) dating from 1310. In addition to the main church, the monastery also has two other places of worship: the church of the Archangels (12th–14th centuries) and the church of St. Nicholas (1834–37), decorated by the renowned icon painter Zahari Zograf (1810–53).

*Above: the **church of the Holy Mother of God at Bachkovo Monastery**, with antechurch and gardens. In the background are the monastery buildings.*

*Left: an icon tablet in the **church of the Holy Mother of God at Rila Monastery**. At the center is the Virgin Mary with the Infant Jesus.*

Bulgaria's third-largest monastery, Troyan, located at an altitude of over 1,300 feet (400 meters) takes its name from an ancient Roman road (the Via Trajani) and was founded by the end of the 16th century at the latest—but possibly as early as the 14th century—by a hermit from Mount Athos.

The monastery survived turbulent times, during which it was repeatedly raided, before eventually escaping the clutches of the local authorities in 1830 and gaining autonomy under the protection of the patriarch of Constantinople. Other than the older chapel of St. Nicholas the Miracle Worker, located to the south of the main monastery complex and containing wood carvings executed by Brother Cyprian in 1794, the buildings are all in the 19th-century Bulgarian National Revival style. The monastery church dedicated to the Dormition of the Virgin was built of stone in 1785 but subsequently remodeled by the monk Constantine of Pechtera in 1835. Colonnades were built along the north and south walls and the remaining external walls decorated with stone reliefs.

This monastery church also houses an icon of the three-handed Mother of God (Bogorodica Trojeručica), reputed to have miraculous powers. In the years 1847–49 the renowned painter Zahari Zograf, his brother Dmitri and other icon painters of the Samokov School decorated the church with around a hundred figures and religious scenes. Zograf also immortalized himself, the 27 monks then living at the monastery, and their abbot in portraits that are still hanging on the walls. Another important item, a wooden iconostasis with representations of angels, creatures and plants, was made in 1838/9 by artists of the Travina School.

As an important center of Bulgarian culture renowned for its book production, from 1870 onwards Troyan Monastery played an important role in the national uprising against the Ottomans. In 1872 the Bulgarian freedom fighter and national hero Vasil Levski (born 1837 and executed by the Ottomans in 1873) established a revolutionary committee here whose members included 80 of the monastery's monks.

Opposite page above: Saint Cyril and Saint Methodius, the Apostles of the Slavs, with the Cyrillic alphabet devised by them in the 9th century. This fresco in the bell tower of the church at Troyan Monastery was painted by the famous celebrated artist Zahari Zograf in 1848.

*Left: view of the church dedicated to the Dormition of the Virgin at the heart of **Troyan Monastery**, which played a key role in Bulgaria's political history.*

*Right: the interior walls and domes of the church at **Troyan Monastery** were completely covered with frescoes by the Zograf brothers.*

Above: the slender, graceful **church of Putna Monastery** *in Moldavia. Stephen the Great was buried here in 1504.*

Right: the cell of St. Daniil at **Voronet Monastery**. *Stephen the Great had pledged to build a monastery for the hermit, should he succeed in driving the Turks out of Walachia.*

The monasteries of Moldavia

The monasteries of Moldavia in southern Bukovina (Romania) were built by Stephen the Great, Prince of Moldavia 1457–1504, who is said to have made a pledge to endow a church for every victory he won over Poland, Hungary, or Turkey. He ended up building 40 churches and monasteries.

Putna Monastery was built between 1466 and 1469 as the spiritual center of Stephen's realm. The monastery church 121 feet (37 meters) long was rebuilt between 1653 and 1662 without exterior frescoes following the destruction of the original complex, of which only the treasury bell tower survives. After sustaining further damage, work started on the reconstruction of the church, during the course of which a west tower was added in 1757. Of particular note is the crypt containing the tombs of Stephen the Great and his wives and sons. Stephen, who was canonized by the Orthodox Church in 1992, endowed the church with numerous precious objects including books, tapestries, an

icon that he carried with him in battle, and the skull of St. Gennadius encased in gold.

Moldavian monasteries are traditionally noted for their exterior frescoes in which scenes from the Bible are presented to the people in the form of picture stories. The most important of these is the women's convent of St. George in Voronet. The convent church was covered with frescoes inside (1535–43) and out (up to 1547) and in 1547 was given an exonarthex (external vestibule) in the Renaissance style by the metropolitan bishop of Moldavia, Grigori Rosca (died 1570).

On the west side of the church the colorful exterior frescoes—dominated by "Voronet blue"—depict the Last Judgment with heaven and the fires of hell, a hand holding the scales of justice and animals among the resurrected dead. The frescoes on the south side depict a Tree of Jesse showing Christ's descent and portraits of the hermit Daniil, to whom Stephen the Great had dedicated the monastery, and Grigori Rosca. The north wall presents a fresco of the Creation and the Temptation of Adam.

*Above: the frescoed exterior of the **church of Voronet Monastery** (south side). The interior of the church contains frescoes of the Last Supper, a portrait of Stephen the Great and the throne of Metropolitan Bishop Grigori Rosca.*

*Left: the **church of Voronet monastery in Moldavia** is sometimes referred to as the "Sistine Chapel of the East" because of the wealth of images covering its walls.*

Orthodox monasteries in Serbia

*View of the main church, dedicated to the Holy Mother of God, of **Studenica Monastery**, showing its tall exonarthex (external vestibule) endowed by King Stefan Radoslav (reigned 1227–34) which provides access to the two side chapels.*

Sopoćani Monastery, close to the city of Novi Pazar in southwest Serbia, was founded in 1265 by King Stefan Uroš I of Serbia (reigned 1243–76) as a burial chapel for him and his family. When he was deposed by his son in 1276 he moved to the monastery as a monk and died there the following year.

The monastery church, dedicated to the Holy Mother of God, is a basilica in the Serb Romanesque style with a raised nave, double blind arcades below the dome, and two side chapels. In 1340 an exonarthex and bell tower were added. The church's partly damaged frescoes, dating from 1272 to 1276, were thoroughly restored in 1926 and are regarded as one of the highlights of Serbo-Byzantine painting. They depict scenes from the Old and New Testaments and also from the life of the Virgin Mary, including a monumental and particularly impressive representation of the Dormition of the Virgin. The frescoes in the apse are of the Holy Spirit descending on the apostles and liturgical celebrations involving Serbia's earliest saint. Those in the narthex (vestibule within the main building) depict a Tree of Jesse alongside scenes from the early ecumenical councils.

Studenica Monastery, built as a royal funerary chapel between 1183 and 1196 by the founder of the Serb nation and Orthodox saint Stefan Nemanja (reigned 1167–96), was to become one of the largest and wealthiest monastic communities in Serbia. The monastery originally had 12 churches of which three survive, along with the refectory of St. Sava.

The centrally sited single-nave church dedicated to the Holy Mother of God with a dodecagonal crossing dome and ornate doorway and windows, was decorated with frescoes in several phases between 1208 and 1568, the earliest of them in the Byzantine mosaic style. One of the most famous is the gold and azure Crucifixion scene on the west wall. Next to the church of St. Nicholas, built in 1220, whose frescoes only survive in part, stands the single-nave church of SS. Joachim and Anne, also known as the King's Church after Stefan Uroš II Milutin (reigned 1282–1321), who endowed it. Small-format frescoes depict scenes from the life of the Virgin as well as portraits of the prophets, apostles, and church fathers.

*Left: a fresco in the **church of SS. Joachim and Anne at Studenica Monastery**, also known as the "King's Church," depicts the presentation of the young Virgin Mary at the temple by her father, St. Joachim.*

*Below: **Sopoćani Monastery** is designed in the Serb Romanesque style; its founder, Stefan Uroš I, reposes in a marble sarcophagus in the monastery church.*

The fortified monastery of Manasija near the Serbian town of Despotovac was built between 1407 and 1418 by the Serb despot Stefan Lazarević (reigned 1389–1427), a vassal of the Ottomans, who broke the power of the nobility and conquered large areas of the Balkans, as his final resting place.

The monastery church, which became a symbol of the Serb national style in the 18th century, has five domes and a triconch design with three semicircular apses forming a trefoil (clover-leaf shape). The church is an example of the work of the Serbian Late Byzantine Morava School, the leading artistic influence at the Serbian court. Resembling a castle from the outside, the monastery, surrounded by defensive walls 40–50 feet (12–15 meters) high, punctuated by 11 watchtowers, developed into an important center of humanist learning thanks to its Resava writing school. The frescoes in the monastery church depicting the miracles of Christ, the prophets, the martyrs, and the soldier saints, are artistically extremely important but are heavily damaged in places. In 1458 the monastery came under Ottoman sovereignty but became a major center of Serb culture again in the 18th century.

Another outstanding example of the work of the Morava School is Kalenić Monastery in the center of the country (near the town of Kragujevac), which was built between 1413 and 1417 by Bogdan, an aristocratic chamberlain to Stefan Lazarević, and his wife Milica. The monastery church, built to a triconch design with a high central dome resting on a high drum and a shallow calotte or blind dome in the narthex, possesses an elegant façade of alternating rows of red brick and white natural stone resembling marble. The rose windows and frames of the doorways and lower windows are decorated with intricate lily and palmette motifs.

Particularly noteworthy among the frescoes is one of the Marriage at Cana. Others depict scenes from the life of the Virgin (in the narthex), soldier saints (in the apse), the disciples at the Last Supper, and the procession of the church fathers (in the sanctuary). Based on the similarity of design, it has been demonstrated with near certainty that Master Radoslav, the creator of the illustrated Radoslav Gospel with its famous depiction of the four evangelists, and his school were involved in the execution of the frescoes. Kalenić Monastery was burned down by the Ottomans in 1788 as a reprisal for the active participation of its monks in the national resistance but was later rebuilt.

Above: the frescoes in the **church of the Holy Trinity at Manasija Monastery** *depict soldier-saints Nestor and Nicetas plus an unidentified third.*

Opposite page: the **church of the Holy Virgin at Kalenić Monastery**. *View from the southeast. The narthex (antechurch) was rebuilt in 1806.*

Left: view of the solid defensive walls of the fortified **monastery of Manasija near the Serbian town of Despotovac**.

Monasteries of the Russian Orthodox Church

*Below left: the **cathedral of the Assumption of the monastery of the Holy Trinity at Sergiyev Posad** was endowed by Ivan the Terrible in gratitude for his victory over the Tatars in 1552.*

*Below right: arrangement of the most important buildings within the precincts of the **monastery of the Holy Trinity at Sergiyev Posad** near Moscow (drawing based on a monastery plan).*

One of the most important and influential of Russian monasteries, the monastery of the Holy Trinity at Sergiyev Posad, northeast of Moscow, was founded around 1340 by the charismatic hermit Sergius of Radonezh, around whom other monks soon gathered.

The first, wooden, complex was burned down by the Tatars in 1408, whereupon stone buildings were erected, including the rather simple cathedral of the Holy Trinity over the grave of St. Sergius (1422), the church of the Holy Ghost (1456), the church of St. Nikon (1548), and the cathedral of the Assumption (1559–85), which has five domes and a chapel annex containing the tombs of Boris Godunov (reigned 1598–1605) and his family.

Most of the monastery buildings, such as the Baroque painted refectory (1686–92), the bell tower (1741–70), and the Metropolitan's Chambers and Czar's Chambers were added in the 17th and 18th centuries. The integration of the craftsmen's quarters into the monastery area resulted in a kind of monastic suburb (Russian: *posad*). Between 1608 and 1610 the monastery, which is surrounded by a wall 4,213 feet (1,284 meters) long with 11 watchtowers, withstood a siege by a Polish-Lithuanian army during which more than 2,000 of its inhabitants lost their lives.

*Opposite page above: the magnificent entrance to the 5,500 square foot (510 square meter) refectory incorporating the **church of St. Sergius at Sergiyev Posad**.*

*Opposite page below: ceiling and lamp of the Moscow Baroque refectory dedicated to St. Sergius at **Sergiyev Posad**.*

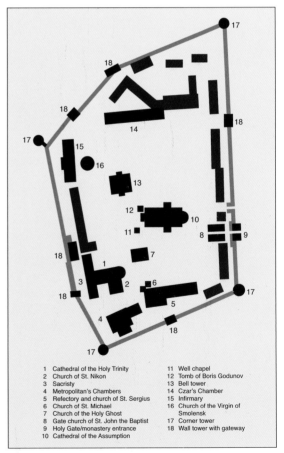

1 Cathedral of the Holy Trinity
2 Church of St. Nikon
3 Sacristy
4 Metropolitan's Chambers
5 Refectory and church of St. Sergius
6 Church of St. Michael
7 Church of the Holy Ghost
8 Gate church of St. John the Baptist
9 Holy Gate/monastery entrance
10 Cathedral of the Assumption
11 Well chapel
12 Tomb of Boris Godunov
13 Bell tower
14 Czar's Chamber
15 Infirmary
16 Church of the Virgin of Smolensk
17 Corner tower
18 Wall tower with gateway

Monks and czars—the struggle for power

After the conquest of Constantinople by the Ottomans in 1453, Moscow regarded itself as the "Third Rome" and the Russian Orthodox Church became the national religion. Monks, particularly those with charisma and miraculous powers, have always exerted a decisive influence over the czars and their politics. Even the autocratic Ivan IV the Terrible (reigned 1533/47–84) heeded their advice.

An early example is Sergius of Radonezh (c. 1319–92), the founder of Sergiyev Posad. Sergius fought passionately for the unification of the Russian principalities under the leadership of Moscow and prophesied the decisive victory of Grand Duke Dmitry Donskoi (reigned 1359–89) over the Mongols in 1380. Although later reforming czars such as Peter the Great (reigned 1689–1725) sought to limit their involvement in politics, monks repeatedly gained positions of influence at court, culminating in the dubious miracle-worker Grigory Rasputin (1869–1916), who held the family of the last czar, Nicholas II (reigned 1894–1917), in his spell. The czar was severely criticised for allowing Rasputin such influence.

Solovetsky Monastery in winter. Although much of the complex is now a museum, a small community of 10 monks has been back here since 1991.

Monasteries in northern Russia

In 1429 the monks Sawaty, Gherman, and Zosima traveled to the inhospitable Solovetsky Islands in the White Sea in northern Russia. There they founded a hermitage named the "New Wilderness," out of which Solovetsky Monastery was created in 1436. After the canonization of its founders in 1547, the monastery became a place of pilgrimage.

Surrounded by thick defensive walls punctuated by seven gates and eight fortified towers, Solovetsky Monastery withstood a number of attacks by Livonian and Swedish armies. Under its energetic hegumen (superior) Philip Kolychev (1548–66), the Uspensky (1552–57) and Preobazhenski (1556–64) cathedrals were constructed at the site as well as a number of other monastery buildings connected by arched passages. To these were added the cathedral of the Annunciation (1596–1601), a water mill, a bell tower (1777), and ultimately the churches of St. Nicholas (1834) and St. Alexander Nevsky.

Having served during the 17th century as a place of refuge for opponents (the "Old Believers") of the church reforms initiated by the Moscow patriarchs, the monastery was later used by the czars as a place of exile and in 1926

acquired notoriety as the first penal camp in the Soviet network of gulags. Another monastery in northern Russia that developed into a center of Russian culture is Ferapontov Monastery in oblast (administrative region) Vologda.

Founded by the monk St. Ferapont in 1398, the first stone building was not erected here until the end of the 15th century, with the main cathedral of the Nativity of the Virgin being completed in 1490. This brick structure was followed in 1531 by the refectory and the cathedral of the Annunciation with bell tower. Richly endowed by the czars, the tent-like church of St. Martinian was added in 1641, followed by the two barbican churches St. Ferapont and the Divine Manifestation in 1650 and the bell tower in 1680.

Between 1502 and 1504 the cathedral of the Nativity of the Virgin was decorated with frescoes by the painter Master Dionysius. These famous paintings extend over some 6,500 square feet (600 square meters) and depict the evangelists, saints, and ecclesiastical councils. Particularly noteworthy is the *Hymn to the Mother of God* (Acathistus) cycle. Ferapontov Monastery was closed down initially in 1798 and later by the Soviet authorities for good in 1924. Since 1975 it has been the site of a museum housing a collection of icons.

Left: Christus Pantokrator, a fresco by the important painter Master Dionysius in the dome of the cathedral of the Nativity of the Virgin at **Ferapontov Monastery**, northern Russia.

Below: the iconostasis of the 16th-century **Preobazhenski Cathedral at Solovetsky Monastery**. The monastery became prosperous thanks to salt production and pearl cultivation and trading.

Monasteries in the Moscow and St. Petersburg regions

Founded by Czar Vassily II (reigned 1505–33) in 1524, Novodevichy (New Maidens') Convent grew to be one of the wealthiest and most important monasteries in the Moscow region, primarily as a result of various female members of the royal and boyar families entering it.

The main cathedral, with five domes and three apses, was built in 1524/5 and dedicated to the Mother of God of Smolensk. Its frescoes were completed in several phases between 1526 and 1666. Also surviving from the early period are the church of St. Ambrose and the refectory. After it was gutted by two fires started by the Crimean Tatars (1571) and the Poles (1611), new buildings were erected on the site, which is enclosed by a defensive wall of red brick punctuated by 12 towers, including 2 gate churches dedicated to the Transfiguration of Christ and the Holy Virgin, a new refectory and monastic building as well as a six-story octagonal bell tower (1689/90). Later in its history the convent accommodated a military hospital and an orphanage. It was dissolved in 1922 and was turned into a museum in 1934. It is now once again the seat of a number of religious institutions.

Novy Ierusalim (New Jerusalem) Monastery in Istra near Moscow was built in 1656 by Nikon, Patriarch of Moscow 1652–58 as his official seat. This pugnacious ecclesiastical politician, who was forced into exile as a result of ongoing conflict with the czars and a schism in the church between the "Old and New Believers" initiated by his liturgical reforms, wanted to outdo the church of the Holy Sepulcher in Jerusalem with this building project.

The main cathedral of the Resurrection, containing the tomb of Patriarch Nikon (died 1681), was built between 1656 and 1685. This was followed by the Patriarch's Residence, the refectory, and other monastery buildings, the church of the Holy Trinity (1686–98) and a perimeter wall with eight towers (1690–94). The entire complex is richly decorated with tiles, majolica (glazed earthenware), and stucco in the Moscow Baroque style. At the time of its secularization in 1764 the monastery had 13,000 serfs. Closed in 1918, Novy Ierusalim has been a museum since 1920. In 1941 the monastery, famed for its valuable book collection assembled by Nikon from the libraries of various other monasteries, was plundered by German troops who also blew up its bell tower and defensive towers.

*Above: the main **cathedral** of the Resurrection at*   ***Novy Jerusalim Monastery in Istra**. In 1991 a small*   *community of monks moved back here.*

*Opposite page: the **church** of the **Virgin**, one of the two gate churches at **Novodevichy Convent in Moscow**. The convent was named "New Maidens' Convent" in order to distinguish it from the "Old Maidens' Convent" in the Kremlin.*

*Right: **Novodevichy Convent in Moscow**, showing the bell tower and cathedral dedicated to the Mother of God of Smolensk. It was to here that Peter the Great banished both his sister, the regent Sophia (deposed in 1689), and his first wife.*

Surrounded by parkland at the end of Nevsky Prospekt in St. Petersburg stands Alexander Nevsky Monastery. After defeating Sweden at Poltava in 1709, Peter the Great founded the monastery the following year on the spot on the banks of the River Neva where the saint Alexander Nevsky (reigned 1236–63) is said to have defeated the Swedes in 1240.

In 1724 the czar had the relics of the grand prince and national hero transferred to the monastery's main Alexander Nevsky Cathedral. The monastery is also the seat of the Metropolitan Bishop of St. Petersburg and Ladogas (Metropolitan Palace) and houses a spiritual academy. Its other churches include the church of St. Sergei and the Holy Ghost, the church of the Mother of God "Joy of All Grievers," and the five-domed cathedral of the Holy Trinity, built between 1828 and 1835. The monastery is also famous for its cemeteries: the Lazarus, consecrated in 1716, in which scientists are buried, and the slightly more recent Tikhvin, the resting place of famous writers and composers.

Monasteries in Ukraine

The monastery of the Dormition at Pochayiv in Ukraine, founded in 1527, achieved greatness after the monk St. Job of Pochayiv (1551–1651) entered it in 1604, was elected abbot, and through the introduction of a strict and ascetic monastic rule (1618) made Pochayiv the center of Orthodox resistance to attempts to catholicize the region.

After being destroyed by the Ottomans in 1675, imposing new buildings were erected in the Baroque style including the Uspensky Cathedral and monks' wings (1771–82). Later additions include the gatehouse (1835), a bell tower 213 feet (65 meters) high and finally the cathedral of the Holy Trinity and another church (1906–12).

In 1720 the monastery was transferred to the Eastern Catholic Basilian monks, but following their support for the Polish Uprising of 1830/1, was raised to the status of Lavra (meaning "colony of monks") in 1833 and given to the Russian Orthodox monks. The monastery has survived some difficult times and was plundered by the Red Army during the turmoil after 1917, and by German troops in 1941.

*Above: **Alexander Nevsky Monastery** is an example of the Baroque architecture of St. Petersburg, on which Peter the Great exerted a decisive influence.*

*Left: the **monastery of the Dormition at Pochayiv** in Ukraine was built on the spot where the Mother of God had appeared to a group of peasants in 1240. A footprint left by her is on view in the Uspensky Cathedral.*

*Opposite page: a cemetery building at **Alexander Nevsky Monastery in St. Petersburg**. Among the graves of numerous artists, writers, and composers in Tikhvin Cemetery are those of Dostoyevsky, Mussorgsky, and Tchaikovsky.*

The founder of monasticism in Russia is widely considered to be St. Anthony of Kiev (983–1073), who founded one of the earliest and most important monasteries, that of the Dormition at Kiev, also known as the monastery of the Caves (Pecherska Lavra).

In 1013 Anthony traveled from Mount Athos and with Brother Feodosy founded a monastery that, despite being badly destroyed during the Mongol invasion of 1238, developed into the spiritual center of the state of Kievan Rus. This immense complex, enclosed by walls, now comprises around 80 churches as well as monastic buildings, towers, and museums, and is divided into two parts: the magnificent Upper Lavra and the somewhat plainer Lower Lavra. The honorary title of "Lavra" was bestowed on the monastery in 1688.

Nearly all of the surviving buildings date from the 17th and 18th centuries. Among the most important are the All Saints, Exaltation of the Cross, and the Nativity of the Mother of God, as well as the Great Bell Tower (1731–45), featuring exterior columns. The last architectural ensemble to be built was the refectory and church of St. Anthony.

The main church of the complex is the cathedral of the Dormition (also known as the Uspensky). Dating originally from 1073, it was continually extended but was burned down by the Mongols in 1238 and the Tatars in 1410. It was later rebuilt in the Baroque style but was again destroyed, probably by the Red Army, in 1941. After being reconstructed between 1998 and 2000, the cathedral has become a national symbol of Ukraine's turbulent past. After the destruction of the cathedral by the Mongols, the gate church of the Holy Trinity, dating from the 12th century, served as the main church. This place of worship was also remodeled in the Baroque style after 1725 and its interior decorated with frescoes.

The artfully appointed caves that give the monastery its name comprise underground monks' cells, chapels, and corridors containing the mummies and sarcophagi of famous monks. They are also divided into two groups: the "Near Caves" (relative to the Upper Lavra) and the "Far Caves" accessible from the Lower Lavra. Brother Nestor (c. 1056–1114), the most important chronicler of Russia's early history, is buried in the "Near Caves." In 1929 the Soviet authorities closed the caves but since 1988 a community of around one hundred monks has reestablished itself at the monastery complex in Kiev.

*Left: the main **Uspensky** (**Dormition of the Virgin**) **Cathedral at the monastery of the Caves in Kiev**, shines with renewed resplendence following its reconstruction between 1998 and 2000.*

*Above: the Great Bell Tower at the **monastery of the Caves in Kiev**, built in the Ukrainian Baroque style, is four stories high and decorated with classical columns. Its largest bell dates from 1903 and weighs 5 tons (4.5 metric tons).*

Monasteries of the Syrian Orthodox Church

*At the center of the ruined main building of the **monastery of St. Simeon, Qal'at Sim'an**, are the remains of a pillar originally 60 feet (18 meters) high surmounted by a 22 square foot (2 square meter) platform on which St. Simeon lived, praying and preaching, for over thirty years.*

M or Gabriel Monastery in southern Turkey, founded in 397 by St. Samuel (died 409) and his disciple St. Simon, is one of the oldest monasteries in Christendom. The abbot of the monastery, which was renowned far and wide for its school and collection of manuscripts, and numbered around 1,000 monks in the 6th century, became bishop of the Tur Abdin (meaning "mountain of the servants of God") region in 615. The monastery takes its name from the miracle-working Bishop Mor Gabriel (abbot 634–68).

The monastery buildings of beige sandstone were erected from the 5th century onwards and the Dome of Theodora, with a diameter of 38 feet (11.5 meters), was completed in the 6th century. Of particular note are the Byzantine mosaics adorning the floors and walls. During the genocide of the Aramaic-speaking Christian Suryoye (Assyrian) people committed by Turks and Kurds under the Ottoman Empire, the monastery was closed (1915–18). Mor Gabriel has been in the headlines since 2008, when the surrounding Kurd villages demanded the demolition of the monastery on the grounds that it was an illegal settlement.

Another monastery in the same region is Mor Hanania, also known as Deir az-Zafaran after the saffron color of its buildings. Mor Hanania was founded either in 493 by St. Eugenius or in 792 by Brother Ananias (Hanania); between 1207 and 1923 it was the seat of the patriarch of the Syrian Orthodox church. Both the church of the Virgin Mary and the monastery's main church, with a pyramid-shaped roof and a funerary chapel containing the tombs of 36 patriarchs, were built during the reign of Emperor Anastasius I (491–518).

In the 5th century, Emperor Zenon (reigned 474–91) built a church and place of pilgrimage of some 2 square miles (5 square kilometers) at the site where the pillar hermit St. Simeon Stylites the Elder (389–459), who was venerated during his own lifetime, had lived for over 30 years on a stone column. Extending in the direction of the cardinal points from the octagonal main room of the monastery of St. Simeon, Qal'at Sim'an, which contains the remains of Simeon's pillar, were four aisled basilicas. From the south portal a path leads to a baptistery with a large font located some 985 feet (300 meters) further south.

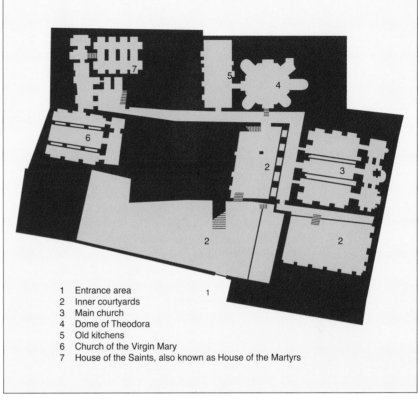

1 Entrance area
2 Inner courtyards
3 Main church
4 Dome of Theodora
5 Old kitchens
6 Church of the Virgin Mary
7 House of the Saints, also known as House of the Martyrs

*Above left: the **monastery of Dei az-Zafaran** is built over the remains of an antique temple. Legend has it that 12,000 martyrs are buried at the site.*

Above right: plan of Mor Gabriel Monastery (drawing from a model).

*Below: **Mor Gabriel Monastery** in southern Turkey is the spiritual center of the Syrian Orthodox Church. Its abbot, Mor Timotheos Samuel Aktas, has been the metropolitan of Tur Abdin since 1985, when the monastery regained its status as an archbishop's seat.*

Monasteries of the Coptic Church

The oldest monastery of the Egyptian Copts dates back to the very beginnings of Christian monasticism. Around 280, the hermit St. Paul of Thebes (c. 228–c. 343) withdrew to a cave in the Nile Valley near Maimun. Not long after, St. Anthony the Great (251–356), who composed the very first monastic rule in 312, moved to a site nearby.

The monastery of St. Anthony (Deir Mar Antonius), founded by Anthony's disciples in 356, takes the form of a monks' village surrounded by walls and is the most ancient Christian monastery still active today. The oldest part of the monastery is its fortified tower where the monks would take refuge during times of danger. The complex possesses seven churches, the main one being St. Anthony's place of burial, whose frescoes, dating from the 10th to the 13th centuries, include the portraits of soldier-saints. The monastery is famous for its library containing over 1,700 old manuscripts. The monks continue to observe a strict and ascetic routine, taking their first meal of the day at midday; on the monastery's 200 fast days, they do not eat until the early evening.

From St. Anthony's Monastery, which has its own corn mill and olive press, 1,158 stone steps lead up some 920 feet (280 meters) to the cave where St. Anthony spent

View of the main burial church of St. Paul at St. Paul's Monastery in the Egyptian desert. The complex, which is surrounded by palm trees, is smaller than the better-known St. Anthony's Monastery.

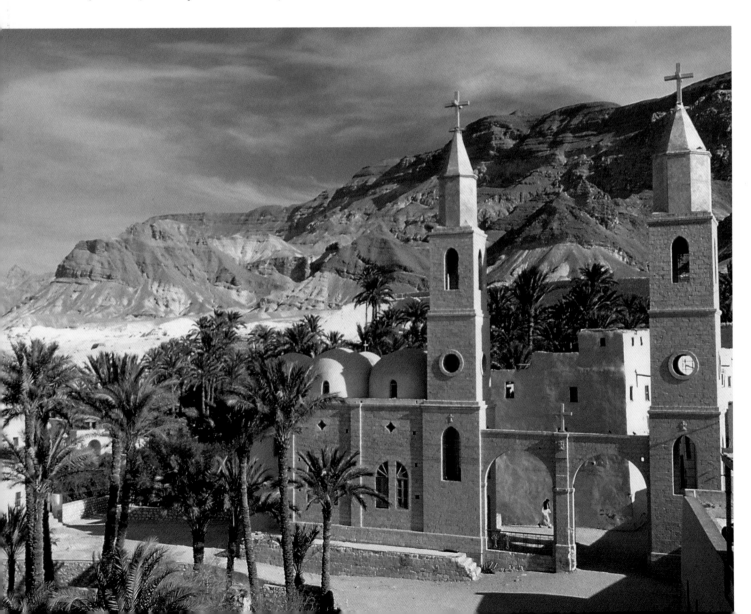

his final years. The monastery was plundered and partially destroyed on several occasions, most recently by Bedouins in 1454. In 1676 the monastery came under the control of the patriarchs of the Coptic Church in Alexandria, who also bear the title of "pope," and remained so for the next 200 years.

The nearby monastery of St. Paul (Deir Mar Boulos), which also has defensive walls and a fortified tower, was built in the 7th/8th century and has four churches, the most recent being the church of St. Michael dating from 1777. The main church, containing the tomb of St. Paul of Thebes on the south side of the nave, is cut into the rock and has three altars beneath painted domes. Its ancient frescoes were painted over and are only now visible in a few places. The monastery was plundered by Bedouins in 1484 and later abandoned for around 120 years before being restored and repopulated by monks from St Anthony's Monastery from 1701 onwards.

Above: the old refectory with table and benches hewn of stone at St. Anthony's Monastery on the Galala Plateau in the Egyptian desert.

Left: narrow channels supply the rooms and gardens at St. Anthony's Monastery in the Egyptian desert with water from a well that rises in a rock niche.

Following the example of St. Anthony and other charismatic desert fathers, in the 4th century a number of saintly monks withdrew to the Scetic Desert near the valley of Wadi an-Natrun, where they and their disciplines formed small communities of hermits. Their leading figure was Macarius of Egypt, also known as Macarius the Great (c. 300–390), and the four surviving monasteries of the Wadi an-Natrun date back to his followers and disciples. These complexes from the 5th and 6th centuries were originally built of wood but after being repeatedly plundered by Bedouin tribes during later centuries were rebuilt in stone. The surviving monasteries are those of St. Macarius (Deir Anba Maqar), St. Borromeus (Deir al-Baramus), the Syrians (Deir al-Suryan), and St. Bishoy (Deir Anba Bishoy). The latter was founded by St. Bishoy (c. 320–417) as an eremitic community and developed into a monastery with a fortified tower and no fewer than five churches surrounded by strong walls.

The original main church and burial place of St. Bishoy in the south of the complex, to which a chapel was annexed in the 11th century, was destroyed during the worst of the Bedouin attacks on the Wadi an-Natrun monasteries (831–48) but was rebuilt around 1330 by Benjamin II, Coptic patriarch 1327–99. The mostly wooden interior of this aisled church with a tripartite sanctuary also dates largely from the time of Benjamin II, whose sarcophagus is to be found in the nave alongside those of St. Bishoy and his followers and St. Paul of Tammah (died 415). The monastery, whose monks' cells are located behind the church of St. Bishoy, possesses three refectories, and the smaller monastery church of St. Iskhirun has a baptistry, accessed by a narrow passage, on the north side of its sanctuary that contains a stone font.

By the 1970s the number of monks living at the monastery had dwindled to 14, but since then it has grown again to over 160. The revival of the monasteries of Wadi an-Natrun is partly due to the efforts of Shenouda III (born 1923), Coptic patriarch since 1971, who made St. Bishoy's Monastery his official seat.

Left above: a fresco in the church at St. Bishoy's Monastery depicts the Virgin Mary and Archangel Gabriel surrounded by the prophets Moses, Isaiah, Ezekiel, and Daniel.

Left below: sandstone church with domes at St. Bishoy's Monastery, one of the four surviving monasteries of Wadi an-Natrun in Egypt.

Opposite page: despite its impenetrable-looking walls, St. Bishoy's Monastery was repeatedly plundered by the Bedouins during its early history, as were the other Wadi an-Natrun monasteries.

Monasteries of the Ethiopian Church

*The **monastery church of Debre Berhan Selassie in Gondar**, seat of the Ethiopian emperors, is named after the "Mountain of Light" (Debre Berhan) on which Emperor Zara Yaqob (reigned 1434–68) founded his capital in 1456.*

For centuries the Ethiopian Church was part of the Coptic Church of Egypt, but Ethiopia—a stronghold of Christianity surrounded by Muslim neighbors—cultivated its own religious life and eventually won its ecclesiastical independence.

The royal seat of Gondar is dominated by the palace complexes (Gemp) and church buildings of its founder Emperor Fasilides (reigned 1632–67) and his successors. Iyasu I (emperor 1682–1706) was responsible for the construction of the richly-decorated monastery of Debre

Berhan Selassie (Holy Trinity on the Mountain of Light). The monastery church takes the form of a rectangular basilica surrounded on all sides by a colonnade and divided into an antechurch (nave for the congregation) and inner sanctum. The interior is completely covered by vibrant wall and ceiling paintings depicting scenes from the Bible as well as from the lives of Christ and the Virgin Mary. The spectacular ceiling beams are painted with winged angels' heads whose large eyes are typical of the Gondar school of painting.

The monastery of Debre Damo, founded around 550 by the saintly monk Abuna or Za Mikael Aregawi, is considered to be Ethiopia's oldest building. Access to the monastery plateau—inhabited by entirely self-sufficient monks—is prohibited to women. Measuring 1,968 x 820 feet (600 x 250 meters), the site is only accessible by rope, which involves being hauled up a sheer cliff 82 feet (25 meters) high. The older of the monastery's two churches is a basilica dating from the 7th–11th centuries whose walls are constructed of alternating courses of wood and limestone. The wooden parts of the building, in particular the coffered ceiling of the narthex, are richly decorated with carvings of animals and mythical creatures. The ceiling of the nave is supported by stone piers transported from Aksum, the ancient Ethiopian center of power, and indeed the entire monastery displays the stylistic influence of Aksumite architecture.

The monastery served as a place of refuge for Emperor Lebna Dengel (reigned 1508–40) and his family during the devastating military campaign of the Muslim sultan of Adal, Ahmad ibn Ibrahim al-Ghazi (1527–43). It was later used as a kind of national prison for imperial princes deprived of power.

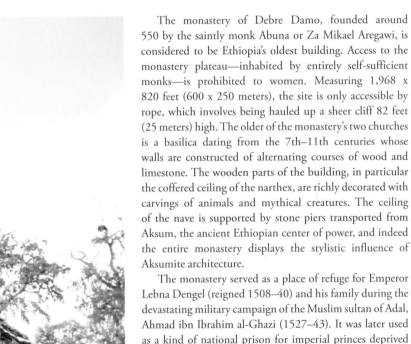

*Above: the church of the almost inaccessible fortified **monastery of Debre Damo**. According to legend, its founder Za Mikael Aregawi was carried up the cliffside by a serpent assisted by angels.*

*Right: the stone entrance and monastic building at the **monastery of Debre Berhan Selassie at Gondar**.*

From the 14th century onwards, monasteries were built on most of the 37 islands in Lake Tana, Ethiopia's biggest lake. With just two exceptions, the monastery churches are rotundas constructed of wood and stone at whose center is a rectangular shrine and inner sanctum. During the military campaign of Ahmad ibn Ibrahim al-Ghazi during the 16th century, valuable manuscripts and other church treasures were brought here for safekeeping.

The monastic fortress on the peninsula of Zeghie was constructed at the beginning of the 17th century—according to tradition by angels and St. George, the hoofprint of whose horse is displayed. The monastery church of Uhra Kidane Mehret was painted at the end of the 19th century with biblical scenes, images of saints, and portraits of benefactors. Among them is the legend of the man-eater Belay, who is saved at the Last Judgment because—despite the atrocious acts he has committed—he gave a beggar water. The monastery has in its keeping four crowns and a coronation cloak said to have been worn by Ethiopian rulers.

The island of Dek, the largest of the Lake Tana islands, possesses no fewer than four monastery churches. Off its western shore lies the island of Narga Selassie, accessible via a stone path during the dry seasons, on which Empress Mentewab (co-regent 1730–55) built a monastery church of the same name whose circular roof is held up by 24 stone pillars.

In around 1750 the church was decorated with paintings of angels and saints, among them a portrait of Empress Mentewab at the feet of the Virgin Mary, in the Gondar style. The church also holds the copy of a famous depiction of Christ wearing the crown of thorns, the *Kwer'at Re'esu* ("The Smiting of His Head"). The original was carried by Emperor Iyasu II (reigned 1730–55) on his unsuccessful campaigns against the Muslims and it was eventually captured by them. In 1868 it fell into British hands, was subsequently auctioned and ended up in private ownership in Portugal. Above the entrance to the church hangs a portrait of the British explorer James Bruce (1730–94), who traveled to Gondar and the monasteries of Lake Tana in 1770/71.

Above: a fresco-like wall painting in the 18th-century Gondar style in the **church of** *Narga Selassie Monastery. Many paintings of this type were fixed to the church wall.*

Right: the inner ambulatory and external wall paintings of the round **church at the monastery of Uhra Kidane Mehret on the peninsula of Zeghie**, *Lake Tana, Ethiopia.*

Opposite page: stone defensive walls punctuated by watchtowers surround the **monastery of Narga Selassie on the island of Dek**, *one of the most important of the Lake Tana monasteries.*

The
Monasteries of
Other Religions

Hinduism
Buddhism
Jainism
Daoism
Islam

Hindu Monasteries

*Previous double page: the enormous palace complex at **Potala Monastery in Lhasa** (Tibet), the seat of the Dalai Lama for centuries.*

*Inset: the many-armed goddess Taleju depicted on a tympanum at **Taleju Temple on Durbar Square in Kathmandu** (Nepal). Taleju, whose blessing was once sought by Nepal's rulers, is believed to be an incarnation of the Hindu deity Durga.*

*Below: monks in prayer in front of a building of the **Vaishnava Monastery on Majuli Island** in the Indian state of Assam.*

Monasticism is just one of many forms of religious life in Hinduism. Hindu monasteries offer an opportunity for retreat from the world during specific phases in life. The traditional *mathas*—Hindu monasteries with their own temple—are inhabited by members of the priestly Brahmin caste who are not celibate, and who do not reside at the monastery for the whole of their lives. They seek withdrawal from the world during a period of self-examination as students (*brahmacarin*). *Mathas* first became established during the 9th century and often have schools, hospitals or orphanages attached to them. Religious leaders (swamis or gurus) are usually the heads of ashrams (see p. 172/3) while religious ascetics such as *sadhus* (a wandering caste) and *rishis* (holy seers who often live as hermits in the forest) are not members of *mathas* of any kind.

Those who live in *mathas* are followers of one of the main Indian gods. There are four main types of *matha*: those of the Vaishnavas, the followers of Vishnu, those of the Shaivas, the followers of Shiva, *mathas* inhabited by the followers of the female goddesses (Shakti) and *mathas* that belong to individual reform movements or newly founded schools and branches within the cult of the main Hindu deities.

Majuli Island in the middle of the Brahmaputra River in the Indian state of Assam is an important center of Hindu monastic life. It was here that the social reformer Srimanta Sankardeva (1449–1568) established a monotheistic cult of Vishnu and exerted a decisive influence on the religious life of Assam though his Mahapuruxiya Dharma religion (approximate meaning: the teaching of a great man in the spirit of the mythical cosmic man Purusha). He and his disciple Madhabdeva are thought to have been responsible for 665 monasteries and hermitages (known as *satras*) in the state of Assam, no fewer than 65 on Majuli alone. Of this number, 22 are still in existence.

Many of these *satras* are famed for their religious crafts; for example, Shamaguri Satra is known for its religious masks. Others are centers of cultural studies or literature or maintain schools or colleges. All the *satras* have developed their own individual dances as a form of religious expression (Sattriya dances or Bongeet Matiakhara) that also date back to Sankardeva. Auniati Satra, for example, one of the four main *satras* on Majuli with 700,000 adherents throughout the world, created the Apsara dances.

Above: lingams at **Jangambari Monastery in Varanasi**. *Lingams are stone phallic symbols representing the regenerative power of the god Shiva. They are decorated by worshippers with flowers and anointed with holy liquids. They stand in a dish (yoni) that symbolizes the female principle.*

Left: view of the interior of a **monastery temple on Majuli Island** *with a statue of a god in a wooden shrine.*

Shankara monasteries

The monasteries founded by Shankara (788–820) display a number of the familiar characteristics of monastic communities. Shankara was the most important thinker of the post-Vedic period and developed the philosophy of Advaita Vedanta (the doctrine of non-duality) that was to exert a major and lasting influence on Hinduism. According to this philosophy, the individual human soul (Atman) is ultimately one with the cosmic soul of the universe (Brahman) and all multiplicity and separateness, meaning that the diversity of the world is illusory (Sanskrit *maya*: illusion). All the gods, including Vishnu and Shiva, are manifestations (incarnations) of the one and only Brahman.

In order to organize and unify the followers of his doctrine, Shankara founded four monasteries in India corresponding to the four cardinal points: Uttaramnaya Matha in Joshimath, Uttarakhand (north), Govardhana Matha in Puri, Orissa (east), Sringeri Sharada Peetham in Shringeri, Karnataka (south), and Dwaraka Pitha in Dwaraka, Gujarat (west). They all became important places of pilgrimage. The oldest and most important is the southern monastery, Sringeri Sharada Peetham, where Shankara is thought to have spent 12 years of his short life as superior.

According to tradition, Shankara and four disciples founded Sringeri Monastery on the banks of the holy River Tunga after receiving a divine sign. Monastic life at Sringeri has been comprehensively documented since the 14th century. The vegetarian gurus (monks) wear ochre robes, rub consecrated ash onto their faces and spend several hours a day in prayer and meditation. They place an emphasis on the study of sacred texts (the Vedas and Shastras), moderation, love of one another, and responsibility towards their fellow gurus.

The superior of Sringeri Sharada Peetham bears the title Jagadguru (Teacher of the World). The current Jagadguru (since 1989), Sri Baharati Tirtha, is the 35th in an unbroken line starting with Shankara. He presides over religious ceremonies wearing a golden crown and seated on a golden throne in the main Sharadamba Temple. Like the three other mother monasteries, the Sringeri complex has been supported by numerous rulers and has been continually extended through the addition of temples and other structures.

*Opposite page: a small temple at the **Advaita Vedanta monastery Sri Shankara Matha in Bangalore** which also belongs to the monastic community founded by Shankara.*

*Below: the west entrance of the Vidyashankar Temple at the **monastery of Sringeri Sharada Peetham**. The temple has a golden dome dating from the 14th century and is decorated on the outside with stone figures of gods and scenes from the Hindu tradition.*

Ashrams

Right: buildings at Sri Aurobindo Ashram in Puducherry. The teacher of Integral Yoga spread the knowledge of Indian sagacity and meditational practices throughout the world.

Below: Rishikesh Ashram on the banks of the Ganges where Maharishi Mahesh Yogi (1918–2008) taught meditation and yoga to—among others—many international artists, including, in 1968, the Beatles.

Better known internationally are India's ashrams, monastery-like meditation centers (Sanskrit *ashram*: place of exertion) where Indian thinkers act as the spiritual leaders (gurus) of unordained followers who do not take lifelong vows.

In 1915 Mahatma Gandhi (1869–1948) founded the Sabarmati or Harijan Ashram in Ahmedabad, Gujarat, which ran schools and bred cattle. Here he developed his philosophy of *ahimsa* (nonviolence) and concept of nonviolent resistance to British colonial rule. It was also from here that he started the famous Salt March through India. His house at the ashram, to which he never subsequently returned, is now a museum, and among other items on display is the spinning wheel at which he taught Indians to make their own clothes, thereby resisting the British import of goods. The ashram in its present form, with educational facilities and a guesthouse, was inaugurated in 1963 by Gandhi's comrade-in-arms Jawaharlal Pandit Nehru.

Perhaps the most important modern ashram is that founded in 1926 by Sri Aurobindo Ghose (1872–1950) in Puducherry (the capital of the Union territory of the same name, an enclave in the state of Tamil Nadu). People were drawn to Integral Yoga, the spiritual path developed by Aurobindo, from all over the world, and by 1950 some 800 disciples were living at the ashram. The complex comprises library buildings, a guesthouse and hotel, kitchens and refectories, numerous workshops and businesses, sports facilities, schools, and a university center, in addition to the main building and courtyard containing the founder's mausoleum (the Samadhi), which is freshly garlanded each day.

After his withdrawal from public life, and officially after his death, the ashram was headed by Aurobindo's spiritual partner Mirra Alfassa (1878–1973, known as "the Mother"). In 1968 she founded the self-governing international township of Auroville, located to the northwest of the ashram, that was laid out in a spiral with Matrimandir Temple (Temple of the Mother) at its center. By 2006 Auroville had 1,829 inhabitants from 40 nations, and in January 2009 the Dalai Lama opened a pavilion of Tibetan culture there.

Buddhist Monasteries

Reflecting the monk-like lifestyle led by the founder of Buddhism, Gautama Buddha (563–483 BC), monasteries with temples and pagodas and monks and nuns have always played an important part in the religion, and in countries such as Myanmar (Burma), Thailand, and Tibet still dominate public life today.

Gautama Buddha achieved enlightenment or awakening (*bodhi*) while meditating under a peepul (*bodhi*) tree in Bodh Gaya (Bihar, India), whereupon he formulated the main aspects of the religion.

This place with its monastery became the main place of pilgrimage for Buddhists. The pyramid-like Mahabodhi Temple (Temple of the Great Awakening) was constructed of brick between the 1st and 3rd centuries. Its base is adorned with 85 statues of the Buddha dating from the 1st century BC while the interior contains a gold statue of the Buddha meditating. To the west of the temple is the Bodhi Tree, in front of which, on the spot where the Buddha attained enlightenment, stands a platform of red sandstone known as the Diamond Throne.

*The **Mahabodhi Temple at Bodh Gaya** (Bihar, India). It was here that Gautama Buddha achieved enlightenment (bodhi).*

Monks and laity—
two paths to nirvana

Tibetan monks at prayer before the Bodhi Tree, where Gautama Buddha attained enlightenment. In the early days, Buddhist monks had to be convinced at special councils that laymen were also capable of achieving nirvana.

Based on the lifestyle of Gautama Buddha, Buddhism was initially a path to enlightenment for monks (the sangha) alone. It was the monks who kept alive the teachings of the Buddha, living their lives in accordance with strict monastic rules (the Vinaya) based on poverty, abstinence, peacefulness and withdrawal from the world. This early form of Theravada or Hinayana (the Lesser Vehicle) Buddhism was not so much a religion as a path towards self-knowledge and a quest on the part of the monks for nirvana.

Thanks above all to the patronage of Emperor Ashoka of the Maurya dynasty (reigned 268–232 BC), Buddhism in its less strict form, Mahayana (the Greater Vehicle), which was easier to integrate into everyday life, also came to embrace laypeople and gradually assumed the aspect of a religion. The figure of the Buddha acquired divine traits and nirvana came to be regarded as a kind of paradise. In contrast to the monks' individual pursuit of nirvana, the Mahayana branch placed an emphasis on compassion and the teachings of the bodhisattvas, enlightened beings who put off their own attainment of nirvana in order to help others along the way.

*Above: ornate wood carvings featuring popular Buddhist imagery at the **palace monastery of Shwendandaw in Mandalay** (Myanmar) which was founded by the Burmese King Mindon Min (reigned 1853–78).*

Monasteries in China

Buddhism is thought to have arrived in China by the 1st century BC but did not achieve widespread acceptance until considerably later. The monk Bodhidharma (died 532) is considered to be the founder of true Chinese Buddhism (known as Chan Buddhism). In 527, Bodhidharma visited the monastery of Shaolin (meaning "young forest"), which had been founded on Song Shan, one of China's Five Sacred Mountains, in the province of Henan in 495. There he taught the monks the basics of Kung Fu (also known as *Shaolin Quan Fa*). The monastery is renowned for its martial arts to this day.

Ever since the Tang Dynasty (618–907), Shaolin has been the center of monastic Chan Buddhism. Its monks increased rapidly in number, growing into an army of 2,500 warriors who served as the bodyguard of the imperial family. During the Yuan Dynasty (1271–1368) the abbot was made superintendent of all China's Buddhist monasteries. The Shaolin monastery complex became famous for its prayer halls, exceeding 5,000 in number, the Temple of the First Patriarch (Bodhidharma), and its forest of pagodas and stele, whose inscriptions date back as far as 549. In the 20th century the monastery fell victim more than once to China's unsettled political situation and was destroyed in 1928 with the loss of numerous texts and other treasures.

Another important monastery is Baoguang in the provincial capital of Chengdu (Sichuan), where the 13-story Sheli Pagoda, which is nearly 100 feet (30 meters) high, was erected in around 1100. Baoguang's prayer halls, particularly the main Arhat Hall, built in 1851, house numerous precious objects including two decorative pagodas over 16 feet (5 meters) high containing relics of the Buddha, a stone tablet incorporating 1,000 carved figures, 59 larger-than-life-sized statues of Buddhas and bodhisattvas, and 518 statues of arhats (saints).

In 1906 a group of monks founded a "Great Dwelling" on Lantau Island in Hong Kong that was elevated to the status of abbey in 1924. The Po Lin (Precious Lotus) site expanded—from 1928 onwards through the addition of the Hall of Perfect Enlightenment, the abbot's chambers and a guesthouse, and from 1932 onwards through the construction of further halls plus a temple and the Lotus Pagoda—into a major monastic center whose abbots were distinguished scholars. The Tian Tan Buddha, an enormous bronze statue 112 feet (34 meters) tall, was raised nearby in 1993 and another smaller bronze Buddha erected in the monastery courtyard in 1998.

*Opposite page: the important **Chan Monastery of Shaolin near Dengfeng (Henan)**, whose monks are renowned to this day for their skill in the martial art of Shaolin Quan Fa (Shaolin skills of the fist) and also for their strict self-discipline.*

*Right: the traditional main hall, the Hall of Perfect Enlightenment, at **Po Lin Monastery in Hong Kong**.*

*Above: the Sheli Pagoda at **Baoguang Monastery in Chengdu (Sichuan)**, which rises to a height of 100 feet (30 meters). During the Ming Dynasty (1368–1644) the top six stories collapsed. They were subsequently repaired but to different specifications, meaning that the pagoda now leans conspicuously to the west.*

*View of **Samye Monastery near Lhasa** showing the golden roofs of its upper stories. Samye is Tibet's oldest monastery and was the mother house of numerous later foundations.*

Monasteries in Tibet

Tibet has come to be regarded as the archetypal land of the monastery and indeed was home to some 6,000 before the destruction wrought by the Chinese Cultural Revolution (1966–76). Buddhism did not reach Tibet until the 6th century but, as in China, it was some time after its initial arrival that it gained widespread acceptance. This only occurred thanks to the efforts of the outstanding teacher and monk Padmasambhava in the 8th/9th century. In a tense relationship with the indigenous Tibetan religion, Bön, which contained a strong shamanistic element, Tibetan Buddhism, known as Lamaism, developed an extensive and highly individual canon of teachings, scriptures and practices based on translations and reworkings. Tantric or Vajrayana

Buddhism (the Diamond Vehicle), of which Lamaism is a branch, incorporates magical practices, the chanting of formulaic prayers (mantras) and the visualization of meditational goals in the form of mandalas (geometrically idealized representations of the so-called Pure Realm), often made of colored sand. From the 11th century onwards, independent, mostly tantric, schools of Buddhism, such as the Kadampa, Kagyu, Nyingma, Sakya, and Gelug schools, started to develop in Tibet. At Padmasambhava's instigation, King Trisong Detsen (reigned 755–97), a strong supporter of Buddhism in Tibet, founded Samye Monastery (meaning "the one that exceeds all expectations"), dedicated to the Buddhist tutelary god Pekar. Samye, Tibet's oldest monastery, was the starting point for the development of the country's monastic movements and an early center of learning.

Above: the Wheel of Law (Dharmachakra), one of the most important Buddhist symbols that is often found above the entrance to Tibetan monasteries. The example *pictured here is at the **Gelug Monastery of Sêra in Lhasa** (see p. 181). The eight spokes represent the Eightfold Path and Four Noble Truths of Buddhism.* *Below: monastery temple and a large stupa at **Samye Monastery** (founded c. 770), where most of the early Tibetan Buddhist scriptures originated.*

The main monastery temple has three stories representing the architectural styles of India, China, and Tibet. At each of its four corners is a large stupa (shrine housing Buddhist relics) and it is surrounded by a circular wall in which a further 108 stupas are set. The temple is surrounded on all four sides by other temples. Samye Monastery has lived through difficult times and was first dissolved under King Longdarma (reigned 836–42), an opponent of Buddhism who defrocked its monks and forced them to return to the laity. The monastery was looted during the Chinese Cultural Revolution (1966–76) but subsequently restored by Tibetans. Today Samye is run jointly by the Nyingma and Sakya schools.

The Gelug school, founded by the reformer Tsongkhapa (1357–1419), developed into Tibet's most powerful

Above: **Gandain Monastery near Dêqên** (east of Lhasa), which is laid out as a self-contained village. Gandain was the seat of the head of the Gelug school of Buddhism. In the foreground are seen characteristic prayer flags attached to long strings.

Right: a wall painting at **Drepung Monastery** depicting a Buddhist deity. Tutelary gods play an important role in Tibetan Buddhism.

religious order. Also known as the Yellow Hat Sect after its monastic headdress, its three most important founding monasteries are Gandain, founded by Tsongkhapa himself in 1409, Drepung, and Sêra, founded in 1416 and 1419 respectively by his disciples.

At Gandain Monastery (Tibetan *ganden*, meaning "continent of perfect victorious happiness"), not only was the main temple built in 1409 but also at the same time more than 70 other buildings. As an important place of teaching and learning of the sutras (main scriptures) and tantras (tantric scriptures), the monastery possessed two *chacang* (faculties) with 13 and 11 *kangcain* (departments) respectively. The three-story assembly hall known as the Lhagyi covers over 21,500 square feet (2,000 square meters). Tsongkhapa's chambers (the founder died at the monastery and his skull is preserved here as a relic) were converted into the Sidongkang Memorial Hall. The abbot (Ganden Tripa), who holds office for a period of seven years, is also the head of the Gelug school of Buddhism. Gandain Monastery, where around 7,500 monks lived and studied in 1959, was completely destroyed during the Cultural Revolution (1966–76) but restored in 1980.

Until 1642 the seat of the Dalai Lama (see p. 183) (see p. 183) was Drepung Monastery, where the government palace (Ganden Phodrang) still survives. As a political center, Drepung has been involved in numerous violent conflicts over the centuries. Its main buildings comprise a central assembly hall plus four halls housing the four monastery faculties, each of which teaches a specific aspect of the Buddhist scriptural and doctrinal tradition. Drepung is Tibet's largest monastery, and until 1959 more than 10,000 monks lived here. It once owned 186 farms and held sway over 20,000 bondsmen and 16,000 herdsmen. In 1985 only 20 monks were living here, although by 2005 this number had risen to 640.

In 1959, 10,000 or so monks were also living and studying at the monastery of Sêra (meaning wild rose). Covering a territory some 44 square miles (115 square kilometers) in area, Sêra comprises 33 faculty buildings and 30 residential buildings. The four-story main assembly hall and administrative center known as the Cogqên covers over 21,500 square feet (2,000 square meters) and houses countless statues. The three faculty halls were built between 1419 and 1559. Sêra Monastery was largely spared during the Cultural Revolution.

*Above: a building at **Sêra Monastery**, one of the three largest founding monasteries of the Gelug school.*

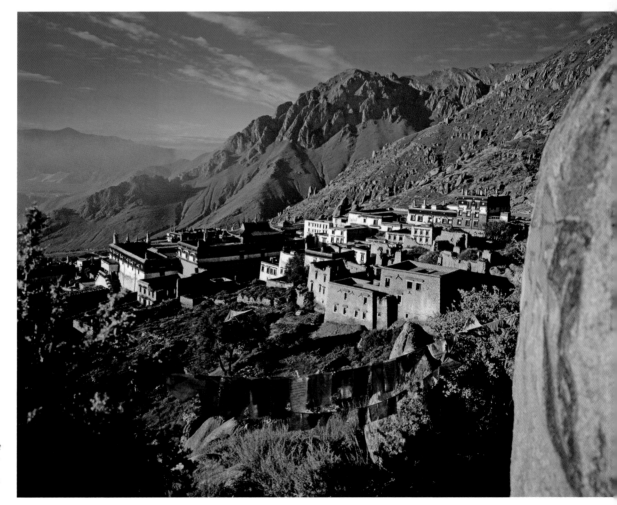

*Right: **Drepung**, Tibet's largest monastery, is another village-like complex and is once again inhabited by hundreds of monks.*

*The enormous monastery complex of **Potala Palace in Lhasa**, for centuries the seat of government of the Dalai Lama.*

Another important Gelug monastery is Zhaxilhünbo (Tashilhunpo) at Xigazê, founded by Gendun Drub (1391–1475) in 1447 and officially consecrated in 1463. Gendun Drub was a disciple of Tsongkhapa who was posthumously recognized as the first Dalai Lama. In 1601 Losang Qoigyi Gyaincain (1570–1662), master of the 5th Dalai Lama, was abbot here and was given the title "Panchen Lama." The main Maitreya Hall at this 46-acre (18.5-hectare) site contains a gold and bronze statue of a seated Buddha Maitreya ("Buddha of the Future") over 85 feet (26 meters) high, as well as the funerary stupas of the 5th to 9th Panchen Lamas.

The largest monastery complex of the Gelug school is the enormous monastery-palace of Potala that sits on a hilltop overlooking the Tibetan capital Lhasa. This was the seat of the Dalai Lama from 1642 until the current head of the Tibetan Buddhists fled into exile in India in 1959. The 999 rooms of the complex, which was extended several times up to 1922, rise up to 13 stories high over 1,148 feet (350 meters) in an east–west direction and over 984 feet (300 meters) in a north–south direction. Of particular note among the splendid funerary stupas of the Dalai Lamas is that of the 5th Dalai Lama, which is three stories and 57 feet (17.4 meters) high.

Above: one of the many white stupas at **Zhaxilhünbo Monastery, Xigazê**, the second-largest city in the Tibet Autonomous Region. The monastery and funerary stupas of the 5th to 9th Panchen Lamas were destroyed during the Cultural Revolution, but were rebuilt from 1982 onwards.

Right: the 14th Dalai Lama, Tenzin Gyatso (born 1935), was enthroned in 1940 and has lived in exile in Dharamsala in northern India since 1959. He was awarded the Nobel Peace Prize in 1989 for his international work in fostering cultural understanding.

The Dalai Lama and the Panchen Lama

Tibet's highest spiritual authorities are the Dalai Lama ("ocean-like teacher") and Panchen Lama ("jewel-like scholar"), although strictly speaking they are only the highest authorities within the Gelug school of Buddhism. Like all Tibet's major abbots and heads of schools, they are regarded as living Buddhas, selected by a commission of monks as the reincarnation of the previous incumbent. Since 1578 the Dalai Lama has also been regarded as one of the highest authorities of Tantric Buddhism in general. In 1642, with Mongolian help, the 5th Dalai Lama, Ngawang Lobsang Gyatso (1617–82), was also made the temporal ruler of Tibet, a position held by his successors up to 1959.

The Dalai Lama and Panchen Lama have traditionally been mutually supportive of one another, but in the 20th century a number of conflicts developed between the two. Whereas the 14th Dalai Lama, Tenzin Gyatso, fled into exile in India in 1959, the 10th Panchen Lama (1938–89) remained in Tibet and came to terms with the Chinese. The 11th Panchen Lama, recognized by the Dalai Lama, has since disappeared, and his replacement, chosen by the Chinese and a number of Tibetan monks, is not recognized by His Holiness.

Wats in Southeast Asia

The Buddhist *wats* found predominantly in Thailand and Cambodia function as monastery and temple complexes for monks as well as places of assembly for both monks and the laity. There are also some *wat* temples without attached monasteries.

Wat Pho, known as the "Temple of the Reclining Buddha," located to the south of the royal palace in Bangkok (Thailand), was built in the 17th century and expanded by King Rama I of Siam (reigned 1782–1809) into an enormous complex. The *ubosot* (main temple room) houses Rama's remains in the pedestal of a statue of the Buddha and is surrounded by the "Jeweled Wall" whose outer side is adorned with 152 square reliefs. The gold-plated statue of the reclining Buddha is 174 feet (53 meters) long. Wat Pho houses a university and also has four *chedis* (reliquary pagodas or stupas) that are 138 feet (42 meters) high and covered by tiled mosaics.

The largest of the 29 *wats* on the island of Phuket, Thailand, is Wat Chalong, a place of pilgrimage with a splendid *chedi* and an *ubosot* in which two 19th-century monk-healers are venerated.

*Right: in its strict geometrical form, the **Angkor Wat** complex represents an idealized Hindu cosmos. The temple, with its lotus-flower towers, of which the central one rises high above the others, symbolizes the sacred Mount Meru at the center of the universe, surrounded by the cosmic ocean represented by the moat (drawing based on a model).*

*Below: view across the moat to the buildings of **Angkor Wat in Cambodia**, the world's largest temple complex. The complex is visited not only by tourists, but also, on a daily basis, by Buddhist monks.*

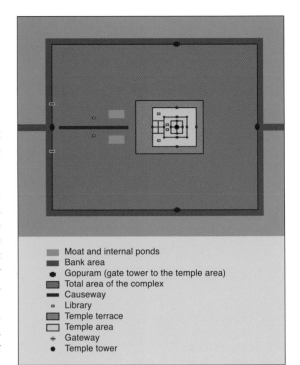

- ▨ Moat and internal ponds
- ▨ Bank area
- ⬟ Gopuram (gate tower to the temple area)
- ▨ Total area of the complex
- ▬ Causeway
- ▫ Library
- ▨ Temple terrace
- ▫ Temple area
- ✛ Gateway
- ● Temple tower

Angkor Wat in Cambodia, a testament in stone to the power and piety of the Khmer Empire that dominated Southeast Asia during the 9th to 15th centuries, is thought to be the largest temple complex in the world. Extending for nearly 1 mile (1.6 kilometers) east to west and north to south, the complex is enclosed by a rectangular moat up to 623 feet (190 meters) wide in places. Angkor Wat was built by King Suryavarman II (reigned 1113–50), a worshipper of the Hindu god Vishnu who had himself depicted in reliefs as an embodiment of Vishnu. The complex was continually expanded by Suryavarman's followers and symbolizes the ideal Hindu cosmos, with Mount Meru (represented by the central temple with its five towers in the shape of lotus flowers, the highest of which rises to 213 feet/65 meters) at its center. Surrounding the temple is a flat relief 2,625 feet (800 meters) long, decorated with various scenes, while other reliefs carved into the building's sandstone walls depict graceful female dancers, the Asparas, each one different. Only later did Angkor Wat become a Buddhist site; the earliest Buddhist wall inscriptions date from 1546. The temple complex has been a major place of pilgrimage for Buddhists ever since.

*Above: gold Buddha statues at the temple of **Wat Pho in Bangkok**, an important Buddhist site in the Thai capital.*

*Left: **Wat Chalong on the island of Phuket** (Thailand), where two monks skilled in the art of healing are venerated. In 1876, Luang Pho Chuang and Luang Pho Chaem came to the aid of injured Thai tin miners during their 1876 uprising.*

Monasteries in Japan

In Japan, Buddhism developed new schools all of its own. One of the leading teachers of the early period was the monk Kukai (774–835), known by the honorary title of Kobo Daishi ("Master of the Spreading of the Law"), who composed key texts, was a political advisor to the imperial family, and founded the tantric-esoteric Shingon sect, which is close in spirit to the ancient Japanese Shinto religion.

In 816, Kukai founded the monastic center of Koya-san (formally consecrated in 819) on a mountain on Kii Peninsula. The main monastery temple of Kongobu-ji remains to this day the chief temple and administrative center of the Shingon sect, and for a long time housed sacred images dating from Kukai's time which were lost in a fire in 1926. The monastery complex also includes Kukai's mausoleum (Okunoin), as well as the main Konpon Daito pagoda that according to Shingon doctrine stands at the center of a spiritual mandala that extends over the whole of Japan.

Another unique development in Japan was the transformation of Chan Buddhism, which had arrived from China, into Zen, a Japanese school of Buddhism in which self-discipline and meditative breathing techniques constitute the core of religious practice—as manifested in *zazen* (seated meditation) and other forms of meditation including archery, the tea ceremony, and garden design. Japan's most famous Zen masters are the monks Eisai (1141–1215), the founder of the Rinzai school (Rinzai-shu), and Dogen (1200–53), the founder of the Soto school (Soto-shu).

One of the most important Rinzai-shu temples is the monastery and temple complex of Daitoku-ji in Kyoto, built between 1315 and 1325. Daitoku-ji comprises a main temple, 22 subsidiary temples, and several gateways and Zen gardens. The Rinzai school has been headed by many important Zen masters. Although Daitoku-ji was burned down during the Onin Wars (1467–77), it was rebuilt and subsequently developed, particularly during the time of the Three Great Unifiers of Japan (1573–1603), into one of the country's most important spiritual centers. Oda Nobunaga (1534–82), the first great unifier, is buried at the site. In the 20th century, Daitoku-ji opened its doors to the first Western practitioners of Zen.

*Left: the **Zuiho-in complex in Kyoto**, founded in 1535, is a dependent temple of Daitoku-ji and is famous for its Zen garden composed of gravel, boulders, and moss. Drawing lines in the gravel with a rake is one of the regular meditational exercises practiced by the Zen monks of Zuiho-in.*

Left: votive tablets, on which the Buddhist faithful write their desires and concerns, at a monastery in Tokyo.

*Opposite page: the mountain monastery of **Koya-san on Kii Peninsula**, Japan, is the seat of the Shingon school of Tantric Buddhism.*

*Left: a minimalist meditation room at the **Rinzai-shu monastery of Daitoku-ji in Kyoto**. Seated meditation is practiced with one's back facing the wall under the Rinzai school, or with one's front facing the wall under the Soto school.*

Jain Monasteries

Like Buddhism, Jainism, founded by Mahavira (599–527 BC), was originally a reform movement of Hinduism and shares a quest for release from the cycle of life, death, and rebirth. In Jainism, monastic life (for both men and women) and monasteries play a very important role. The monks (*muni*) and nuns (*sadhvi*) are divided into the strictly ascetic Digambaras (the "clothed in air"), who wear no clothes, or only a loincloth, and practice nonviolence toward all living creatures (*ahimsa*), and the less strict Shvetambaras (the "clothed in white"), who are allowed to have personal possessions and engage in business.

The monastery and temple complex of Pawapuri, some 62 miles (100 kilometers) from Patna, the capital of the Indian state of Bihar, is the holy site of the Jains. It was here in the Gaonmandir Temple that Mahavira attained nirvana (*moksha*). His corpse was cremated and his ashes preserved in a large stupa. The central temple of Jalmandir, built of marble, is located in the middle of a lake strewn with lotus flowers, and is accessible across a stone bridge. The complex has five main temples, including Samosharan Temple where Mahavira instructed his disciples toward the end of his life.

*View across the lotus-flower-strewn lake toward the central **Jalmandir Temple** at the monastery and temple complex of **Pawapuri** (Bihar).*

Perhaps the most important Jain building is the Ranakpur complex in the Aravalli Mountains (Rajasthan), which was built during the 14th and 15th centuries. Jains believe that mountains are the holy realm of the 24th Tirthankaras (world teachers), the last in the line being Mahariva. The main temple at Ranakpur is dedicated to the first Tirthankara, Adinatha, who stands at the very beginning of human history. It is classed as a four-faced (Chaumukha) temple because the central statue of Adinatha—in a main room surrounded by an ambulatory—looks in all four directions. The entrance to the temple takes the form of a three-story portal, up to which a flight of stone steps leads. The halls of the temple are surmounted by domes and high roof towers. The courtyard contains smaller, colonnaded temples; the complex as a whole possesses 1,444 columns. Its walls are covered from top to bottom with figurative reliefs.

The smaller temples to the 23rd Tirthankara, Parshvanatha, and the 22nd, Neminatha, are also covered with rich decorative figure work.

Left: view of the exterior of the main Adinath Temple at the temple complex of Ranakpur (Rajasthan) with its numerous roof towers.

Below left: a stone elephant surrounded by exquisitely crafted marble pillars inside Adinath Temple at Ranakpur.

Below right: stone relief depicting dancers on one of the temples at Ranakpur. Jain buildings are renowned for their exquisite relief work and figures.

Daoist Monasteries

onks and monasteries also play an important part in Daoism, one of China's great philosophical traditions. In terms of their ideals and organization, Daoist and Buddhist monasticism have much in common, although because of the importance of nature to Daoist thinking, its monasteries are more frequently built in difficult-to-reach spots—on the tops of high mountains, for example. The Daoist school of Neidan (Quanzhen), which started to develop in the 12th century, built monasteries for celibate and abstinent monks and nuns who dedicated themselves to lengthy meditations, breathing techniques ("internal alchemy"), and a wide range of health-related exercises.

Daoism regards the Wudang Mountains (Wudang Shan) in the province of Hubei, with their 72 peaks, as the most sacred mountain range on earth. From the 3rd century onwards, hermitages of the various Dao schools were established here, and in the 15th century an independent school of Wudang Daoism developed. Emperor Yongle (reigned 1402–24) sponsored the building of around 130 monasteries with temples, bridges, and gateways in the Wudang mountains. Of particular note is the Purple Clouds Palace (Zixiaogong), constructed on four different levels of the mountainside, whose main hall (the Zixiaodian) houses the statue of the "Perfect Warrior."

*Above: a temple hall at the extensive site of the **Temple of White Clouds in Beijing**. Incense is burned in the sacrificial vessel that stands before it. The complex was badly damaged during the Chinese Cultural Revolution (1966–76) but was restored in 2000.*

A man-made path leads up to the highest peak, Tianzhu (Pillar of Heaven), at 5,250 feet (over 1,600 meters), on whose summit the Jindian (Golden Hall) stands. Inside it are figures, sacrificial tables, and the statue of the "Great Perfect Warrior," Zhen Wu.

The 23-square-mile (60-square-kilometer) site of Baiyun Guan (Temple of the White Clouds) in Beijing is the main seat of the Neidan school and also of the Chinese Daoist Society. The first temple building was erected under Emperor Kaiyuan (reigned 713–41) and the monastery founded in 1227. Most of the buildings date from the 16th century. The site has five main halls housing statues and idols. The second most important hall is dedicated to the Jade Emperor—the highest Daoist deity—and the fourth to the great Dao master Qiu Chuji (1148–1227), who lived and was buried here. The monastery possesses a stone tablet containing the text of the *Dao De Jing* (Way of Power), by the legendary founder of Daoism Laozi (6th century BC).

*Opposite page left: view from a mountain peak of the snow-covered monastery buildings of the **monastery complex of Wudang Shan** in the Chinese province of Hubei.*

*Right: steps and incense vessel in front of one of the many temples at **Wudang Shan**.*

*Below: a building at the **monastery and temple complex of Wudang Shan**.*

Monasteries
in Islam

In Islam, monasteries and monastic orders play a less prominent role than in Christianity or Buddhism because withdrawal from shared religious practice as part of the community of the faithful is regarded as an ideal only in exceptional cases. During the early times, however, performing periodic service as a "frontier guard" (Arabic: *murabit*) in a ribat was regarded as a commendable religious act. The *ribats*—castle-like fortified monasteries located in exposed positions on the frontier between the Muslim (*Dar al-Islam*: house of Islam or peace) and non-Muslim spheres of influence (*Dar al-Harb*: house of war)—were manned by defenders of Islam who led ascetic lives dominated by prayer and military service. The Berber Almoravid dynasty in particular, however, used their *ribats* as base camps for a systematic Islamization of West Africa from 1042 onwards.

From Spain to the coast of North Africa, the *ribats* formed a defensive cordon against the Christians—especially in Tunisia. In Sousse the foundations were laid in around 800 of a square *ribat* with sides 130 feet (40 meters) in length. In 821 the structure was completed with the raising of a round tower 90 feet (27 meters) high.

The lower stories around the inner fountain courtyard were once weapons stores, stables, and an oil press, while the upper floor is divided into monks' cells. On one side is the mosque comprising a prayer hall with 11 aisles, a *mihrab* (prayer niche), and a barrel vault. The only entrance to the *ribat* is a double gateway flanked by antique columns in the southern side facing the town.

Significantly larger than the *ribat* at Sousse is that at Monastir (the name of this Tunisian town is thought to derive from the Greek *monasterion*: monastery) built in 796 in order to defend the region from the Byzantine fleet. Originally square, with the monks' cells on the lower story and a small mosque in the southeast wing on the upper floor, in the 9th century a women's *ribat* was added to the south and west, and in the 11th century additional wings were constructed to the north and east, resulting in an interlocking complex. Here too there is a high, conical round tower that was able to communicate with the Sousse *ribat* by means of beacons. Immediately next to the *ribat* are a small Great Mosque, dating from the 9th century, and the foundations of another *ribat* (Sidi Douib).

The monasteries of the Sufi orders

Comparable with the monasteries and orders of other religions are the *tekkes* (places of retreat and protection) of the Sufi orders, which developed out of Islam's numerous religious brotherhoods (Arabic *tariqa*: shared path to God). Sufis are Islamic mystics named after their woolen cloaks (Arabic *suf*).

The main ceremony of all the Sufi orders is the remembrance of Allah (*dhikr*), the repetition of the 99 names of Allah in a rhythmic, ritualistic chant, frequently accompanied by dances or rhythmic movements that can intensify into an ecstatic trance. Sufis believe that Allah inhabits the hearts of all men. Through the practice of *dhikr* ceremonies, participants gradually perfect themselves until they feel a sense of inner oneness with God, a goal that has always been seen by the Islamic orthodoxy as rather suspect.

Each *tekke*, the first having been founded in Damascus in 767, possesses a main hall for *dhikr* ceremonies and ritual prayer, a number of other relatively large rooms for the Sufis and an accommodation wing for the master of the order (sheikh). Some also incorporate social institutions such as a hospital or infirmary.

Above: the buildings of **Mevlevi Tekke in Konya** *(Turkey), the most conspicuous feature of which is the türbe or funerary tower, covered with turquoise tiles, that rises above the sarcophagus of Jalal ad-Din Rumi.*

Right: the magnificently crafted sarcophagus, crowned with a turban, of the founder of the order. This is the main place of worship at **Mevlevi Tekke**.

One of the most famous of the Sufi orders was founded in Konya, Turkey, by the mystic and poet Jalal ad-Din Rumi (1207–73), known as "Mevlana" (Our Master). The members of the Mevlevi order, known in the West as the "Whirling Dervishes," practice *dhikr* by twirling continually around their own axis to rhythmic music played on flutes and drums while wearing long, dress-like robes.

Eleven years after his death, a group of Rumi's disciples founded the Mevlevi Tekke, which is now a museum. This extensive complex comprised a number of wings and an inner courtyard with fountain grouped around a high turquoise *türbe* (funerary tower) of ribbed design. In addition to Rumi, this tower also contains the sarcophagi of a number of his successors as sheikhs of the order. The monastery was dissolved in 1927 by Kemal Atatürk, but remains a place of pilgrimage today and contains numerous manuscripts and precious objects such as prayer carpets, Qu'ran desks, and historical musical instruments.

*Left: the entrance to the mausoleum of the order's founder, Jalal ad-Din Rumi, at the **Mevlevi Tekke** in **Konya**.*

Dervishes

Members of the Sufi orders are generally referred to as "dervishes." The Persian word *darvish* used to describe an ascetic Sufi also means "beggar," indicating the contempt for worldly possessions and embracing of "poverty before God" of the members of such orders. Some dervishes perform ascetic exercises and take an oath of poverty as a sign of *dhikr*, the inner turning to Allah. Because of their wisdom, unconventional lifestyles, original outlook, and poetic gifts, dervishes are often revered by the faithful as mediators between this world and the next.

Whirling Dervishes in the main hall of the Mevlev Tekke in Konya. Their white, shroud-like garments and high caps symbolizing tombstones are signs that they have abjured the world.

The mausolea of the Sufi masters

The Sufi orders became powerful above all in the Ottoman Empire and its sphere of influence. As a result of donations by their members and supporters, they often acquired extensive land holdings and built magnificent *tekkes* and colleges. Two of the most influential Sufi orders were the Bektashi, founded in the 13th century and active mainly in Anatolia, and the Naqshbandi, which had centers in Turkey, Persia, and Central Asia.

The mausoleum (*dargah*), erected at the place where the founder of an order, an important Sufi sheikh, or a Sufi poet had lived and died, would normally be of exquisite design and construction, and would often form the center point of a complex of buildings comprising a mosque, *tekke*, or Qu'ran school (*madrasa*). Mausolea of this kind would be regarded as holy sites by the members of the relevant order and would become a place of pilgrimage for other believers, who venerated numerous sheikhs as miracle-working saints.

The Sufi mystic Ahmed Rifai (1118–81) was the founder of the Rifai order, whose members became known as the "Howling Dervishes" because of their ecstatic *dhikr* practices. The magnificent Al-Rifai Mosque, covering a surface area of 322 x 236 feet (98 x 72 meters), was raised at the site of his tomb (*zawiyah*) in Cairo between 1869 and 1912. In charge of its completion from 1905 onwards was the Austrian architect Max Herz. The interior was based on that of the neighboring Sultan Hassan Mosque, dating from the 14th century. It has magnificent wooden ceilings and uses 19 different types of marble.

*The famous ensemble of mosques in Cairo. From left to right: the **Al-Rifai Mosque**, in honor of the founder of the Rifai order, the **Sultan Hassan Mosque** dating from the Mamluk period, and the great **Alabaster** or **Muhammad Ali Mosque** from the 19th century.*

In addition to the tomb of Rifai next to the south entrance, the mosque's crypt also contains the sarcophagi of almost all the members of Muhammad Ali's family, who ruled Egypt as khedives (viceroys) and kings during the period 1805–1952.

Particularly widespread on the Indian Subcontinent is the Chishti order, founded in the 10th century, whose most important member was Sheikh Khwaja Muid ud-Din Chishti (1141–1230). In the *tekkes* of this order, known as *khanqahs*, absolute equality is practiced, extending to all members including students. The order is financed by public donations alone. The lavish mausoleum of Muid ud-Din Chishti in the Indian city of Ajmer (Rajasthan) remains an important center of pilgrimage today.

Above: the mausoleum (dargah) of the Sufi mystic and order sheikh Muid ud-Din Chishti, an important place of pilgrimage, in Ajmer (Rajasthan, India).

Right: the interior of the cupola above the tomb (the Hafezieh) of the highly revered Sufi poet Hafez (c. 1320–90) in the Musalla Gardens of his home town Shiraz (Iran).

Monastery ground plans

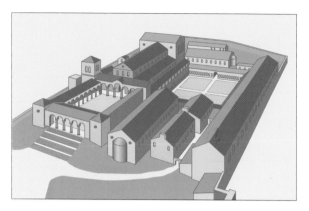

Reconstruction of the abbey of Monte Cassino, the mother monastery of the Benedictine order, in its early days → p. 14

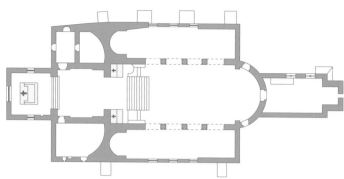

Ground plan of the Benedictine abbey church of St. George at Reichenau-Oberzell → p. 26

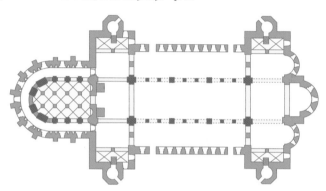

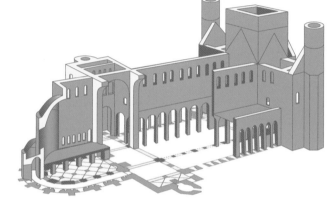

Ground plan and longitudinal section of the Benedictine abbey church of St. Michael in Hildesheim (both showing the state of construction in 1033) → p. 31

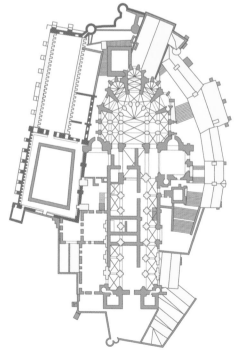

Ground plan of the Benedictine abbey of Mont-Saint-Michel → p. 34

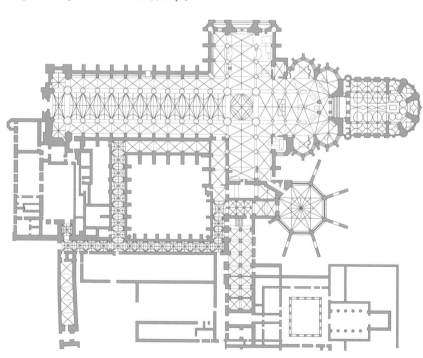

Ground plan of Westminster Abbey, another Benedictine foundation → p. 45

Typical layout of a Cistercian abbey

1–7	Church	16	Auditorium
1	Presbytery	17	Monks' latrines
2	Door to cemetery	18	Calefactorium
3	Monks' choir	19	Lavatorium
4	Choir of the sick and infirm	20	Monks' refectory
5	Choir screen	21	Reading room
6	Lay choir	22	Kitchen
7	Narthex (paradise)	23	Serving hatch
8, 14	Staircase to monks' dormitory	24	Lay brothers' conversation room
	(above 9, 10, 13–16)	25	Lay brothers' refectory
9	Sacristy	26	Lay brothers' latrines
10	Armarium	27	Passage with staircase to lay brothers'
11	Monks' entrance		dormitory (above 25, 27, 28)
12	Cloister with reading chairs	28	Cellar for storage
13	Chapter house	29	Lay brothers' corridor
15	Conversation room (parlatorium)	30	Lay brothers' entrance

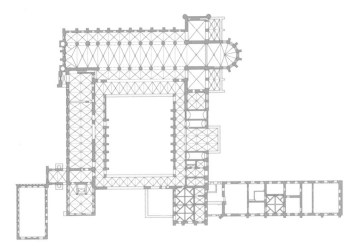

Ground plan of the Cistercian abbey of Chorin → p. 55

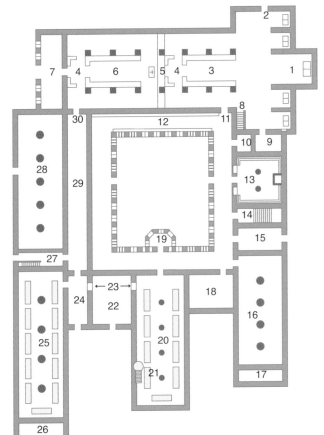

Basic layout of an abbey of the Cistercian order with description of the individual rooms and buildings

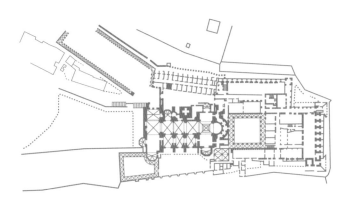

Ground plan of the monastery complex and monastery church of San Francesco in Assisi (Italy), the mother monastery of the Franciscan order → p. 61

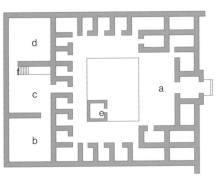

a: Main gateway
b: Assembly room
c: Kitchen
d: Refectory
e: Wash room
f: Staircase to upper story

Basic ground plan of an early Buddhist monastery (vihara): Bhamala in Taxila (northern Pakistan)

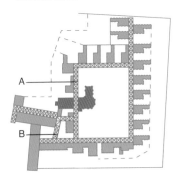

A: Large cloister connecting the hermits' lodgings to the church

B: Small cloister connecting the various communal rooms

a: Large cloister
b: Entrance passage
c: Anteroom
d: Storage room for wood, doubling as a workroom
e: Lavatory
f: Study and bedroom
g: Prayer room

Basic ground plan of a monastery of the Carthusian order

Ground plan of a monk's cell and garden in a Carthusian monastery

Glossary of monastery architecture

In keeping with the main focus of the book, only terms relating to Christian monastic architecture are listed below.

Apse (Greek *apsis*: vault, curve, arch): semicircular or polygonal altar niche in temples or churches, covered by a semidome. Originally an area set aside for priests and bishops, in the 9th century the apse was incorporated into the choir.

Arcade (Latin *arcus*: arch): arches or rows of arches supported by columns or pillars. An antique stylistic element employed in Romanesque church architecture both externally and internally, for example in a basilica to divide the aisles from the nave while allowing them to remain visually and acoustically connected. Arcades set against solid walls are called blind arcades.

Barrel vault: ceiling vault with two parallel springing points of equal length. Springing points are the structural elements that receive and support the lateral and in some cases vertical thrust—of a ceiling in this case. The uppermost portion of the springing point on which the ceiling rests is called the impost.

Basilica (Greek *basiliké*: royal hall): a church whose central nave is higher than its side aisles and has its own windows in the upper portion of its walls (clerestory) above the aisle vaults.

Brick Gothic: Gothic style of architecture employed in particular for churches, monasteries, and public buildings which uses (mainly red) brick as its chief material. Common in northern Germany and the Baltic region between the 12th and 16th centuries.

Buttressing: late antique stylistic element perfected structurally and aesthetically during the Gothic era. A system of (generally external) loadbearing elements, including flying buttresses and counterforts, projecting from the walls of a building in order to counteract the lateral thrust of a ceiling vault.

Capital (Latin *capitellum*: little head): top, usually wider section of a column. Capitals are often decorated with plant motifs (acanthus, lotus, lily), while in the Middle Ages faces, figures, and scenes were common.

Chapel (Latin *cappa*: cape or cloak): within the context of monasteries and the Catholic Church, usually a smaller place of worship for the use of a specific community and without church status under ecclesiastical law. Later, chapels served as holy sanctuaries for specific functions (baptism, adoration of the Blessed Sacrament, funerary chapel). Large churches often have a number of side chapels dedicated to individual saints.

Chapter house: main place of assembly of a monastic community. Usually the room in which abbots were elected and religious vows taken.

Choir (also presbytery): chancel or altar area of a church (in front of the apse), normally east of the nave and reserved for the clergy (Greek *presbuteros*: elder, priest). In Cistercian churches the monks' choir is divided from the lay brothers' choir by a choir screen.

Cloister: vaulted walkway around a monastery's central courtyard or garden with arcades giving onto the central space. The cloister generally connected the monastery church with various other monastery buildings and was used for prayer as well as serving as a cemetery. The cloister is thought to have developed either from the early Christian narthex or from the inner courtyard of Roman villas.

Compound pier: a pier of square or cruciform profile whose core is enclosed by (non-loadbearing) blind, demi-, or three-quarter shafts.

Convent (Latin *conventus*: assembly, company): originally the foregathering of all the full members of a monastery. Later came to denote the entire estate occupied by a religious community.

Crossing: square space formed by the intersection of the nave and transept of a church. The crossing separates the nave from the choir.

Crossing dome: Romanesque stylistic element, a dome or cupola crowning the crossing.

Crossing tower: stylistic element found in Norman and English Gothic churches, a tower surmounting the crossing.

Crypt (Greek, meaning hidden): an underground burial place accessible via steps and located usually below the east-end choir, or altar of a church.

Dormitory (Latin *dormitorium*: sleeping room): the monks' sleeping quarters. In early monasteries only the abbot would have his own room while the monks slept in a communal dormitory. Individual monks' cells (Latin *cella*: small room) were introduced at a later date by canons.

Frieze: a narrow band whose function is to delimit, articulate or embellish certain parts of a building, often taking the form of a decorative and continuous geometric pattern (scrolls, lozenges, crenellations, acanthus, meanders, etc.).

Groin vault: ceiling vault consisting of (at least) two intersecting masonry barrel vaults.

Hall church: a church with nave and aisles of equal height sharing the same saddleback roof.

Icon (Greek *eikón*: picture, likeness): holy image used in the Orthodox and Eastern Christian Churches and forming the central element in Eastern liturgy. Icons have their roots in images believed to have the power to work miracles, and usually depict Christ, the Virgin Mary, or the saints. The controversy over whether or not images should be revered resulted in the Byzantine Iconoclasm (726–842).

Iconostasis: a screen, usually of gilded wood, bearing icons. In Orthodox churches the iconostasis separates the nave and therefore congregation from the sanctuary and priest. An iconostasis has three doors: a central double door known as the Royal Doors, adorned with images of the evangelists, the Virgin Mary or Archangel Gabriel, and the east and west doors featuring depictions of the archangels.

Katholikon (Greek, meaning general, universal): the main church in Greek Orthodox monasteries, generally the largest place of worship of a monastery complex. The *katholikon* generally possesses a narthex and a cathedra (bishop's throne).

Keystone: a Gothic stylistic element: a stone, generally of ornamental design, positioned at the intersection of the ribs of a rib vault.

Lay brothers' wing: the accommodation of a monastery's lay brothers or *conversi*, who were unordained and had a lesser duty of prayer. The lay brothers were the monastery's manual workers, most importantly carrying out any building work, but also looking after the farms, gardens, and granary. The lay brothers came under the jurisdiction of the abbot and cellarer (person in charge of the food and drink) of the monastery.

Narthex (Greek, meaning small box): rectangular, single-story vestibule of a basilica extending across the full width of the church. Usually at the west end, it is separated from the church proper by arcading. A narthex can either be within the church as an esonarthex or without, preceding the façade, as an exonarthex. This space was originally used for baptisms, and in monastery churches is also known as a paradise.

Nave: the main body of a church, where the (lay) congregation worships. Traditionally a longitudinal, rectangular structure separated by columns, piers, or arcading from one or two aisles on either side.

Pointed arch: a key Gothic stylistic element: an arch rising to a point, used most conspicuously in church windows. The pointed arch superseded the Romanesque round arch.

Portal: imposing entrance to monasteries, churches, or palaces, often incorporating columns and a tympanum or figurative scenes.

Portico (Latin, meaning hall): roofed space, either open-sided or partly enclosed, preceding the entrance to a church or house.

Refectory (Latin *refectio*: restoration, recovery): dining room of a monastery, often serving additionally as the place of assembly of the monks or nuns.

Rib vault: a key element in Gothic architecture. Instead of four round arches forming the four sides of a square, the diagonals of a square unit of the vault are described by two round arches (ribs) sharing a single keystone.

Roof turret: low, slender tower or spire that often serves as a bell cage. Unlike a church tower proper, roof turrets do not have their own foundations, but are fixed by means of posts to the roof trusses. Roof turrets were developed in the 13th century by the Cistercian and mendicant orders whose churches—in keeping with their ideal of architectural simplicity—had no towers.

Rose window: circular window above the main door of Gothic churches, often of impressive size and elaborately composed of colored glass and tracery; usually strictly symmetrical and made up of concentric circles. The rose window symbolizes divine perfection and the love of God that radiates from the center equally in all directions.

Round arch (semicircular arch): stylistic element used from antiquity up to the Romanesque era, a semicircular arch of exactly 180 degrees used for windows and doors.

Sanctuary (Latin, meaning shrine): chancel, or altar area (choir), and apse of a church reserved for the clergy. Also the place in monastery libraries where secret writings were kept.

Scriptorium (Latin *scribere*: to write): writing room of a monastery in which—during the Middle Ages in particular—texts were copied and illustrated.

Tracery: filigree stonework used to decorate church windows (particularly the upper part) and parapets, adopting a range of forms and patterns. Perfected during the Gothic era.

Transept: shorter arm of a church positioned at right angles to the nave, resulting generally in a cruciform ground plan. The point of intersection between transept and nave is known as the crossing.

Tympanum (Greek *tympanon*: hand drum): decorative panel occupying the space within a triangular pediment or above doorways. A stylistic element already found in antique temples, in Christian churches the term denotes the semicircular area between the top of the door and the door arch. Often decorated in the Middle Ages with figurative scenes—usually depicting Christ the Almighty at the Last Judgment, separating the righteous from the damned.

Westwork: an independent element preceding the main church building, often of fortified appearance and common above all in imperial abbeys of the Carolingian period. Westworks were usually surmounted by three towers: a higher central tower flanked by three lower ones. They were often used by traveling rulers as a temporary chancellery or court of law and incorporated a royal gallery giving onto the interior of the church behind. Westworks were by and large superseded by other façade designs from the Ottonian period (919–1024) onwards. The oldest surviving westwork is that of Corvey Abbey (Germany).

Monasteries

included in UNESCO's World Heritage List*

EUROPE

Austria:
Gottweig Abbey (2000) → p. 92
Melk Abbey (2000) → p. 93

Belgium:
The beguinages of Flemish towns and cities (1998) → p. 76

Czech Republic:
Historic center of Prague with Jesuit church and monastery (1992) → p. 82

France:
Mont-Saint-Michel and abbey (1979) → p. 35
Abbey church of Sainte Marie-Madeleine in Vézelay (1979) → p. 34
Fontenay Abbey (1981) → p. 48

Germany:
Michaeliskirche (monastery church of St. Michael), Hildesheim (1985) → p. 31
Lorsch Abbey (1991) → p. 30
Monastic island of Reichenau and Reichenau Abbey (2000) → p. 26

Great Britain:
Fountains Abbey (1986) → p. 56
Westminster Abbey (1987) → pp. 44–45

Greece:
Mount Athos and monasteries (1988) → pp. 132–35
Metéora monasteries and cliffs (1988) → p. 128–131
Daphni, Hosios Loukas, and Nea Moni on Chios (1990) → p. 123–25
Monastery of St. John with Cave of the Apocalypse and old town on Patmos (1999) → p. 122

Ireland:
Rocky island and monastery of Skellig Michael (1996) → p. 18

Italy:
Basilica of San Francesco and sites associated with St. Francis at Assisi (2000) → pp. 60–63

Malta:
City of Valletta and castle of the Knights Hospitaller (1980) → pp. 72–73

Poland:
Marienburg (castle of the Teutonic Order) in Malbork (1997) → p. 75

Portugal:
Monastery of St. Jerome in Lisbon (1983) → pp. 12, 78–79
Monastery of Santa Maria da Vitória in Batalha (1983) → p. 81
Templar castle and Convent of Christ in Tomar (1983) → pp. 70–71

Romania:
Seven churches and monasteries in Moldavia, including Voronet (1993) → pp. 140–141

Russia:
St. Petersburg, city center and Alexander Nevsky Monastery (1990) → pp. 152–153
Monasteries on the Solovetsky Islands (1992) → pp. 148–149
Monastery of the Holy Trinity at Sergiyev Posad near Moscow (1993) → pp. 146–147
Ferapontov Monastery, Vologda (2000) → p. 149
Novodevichy Convent in Moscow (2004) → pp. 150–151

Serbia:
Town of Stari Ras with Sopoćani Monastery (1979) → p. 143
Studenica Monastery (1986) → pp. 142–143

Spain:
Historic center of Ávila with Carmelite convents (1985) → p.79

Switzerland:
St. Gallen Abbey (1983) → p. 25

Ukraine:
Cathedral of St. Sophia and Monastery of the Caves (Pecherska Lavra) in Kiev (1990) → pp. 154–155

AMERICA

Argentina:
Jesuit buildings in the Córdoba region (2000) → p. 85

AFRICA

Egypt:
St. Catherine's Monastery on Mount Sinai (2002) → pp. 118–119

Tunisia:
Historic center of Sousse with *ribat* and Great Mosque (1988) → p. 193

ASIA

Cambodia:
The various sites at Angkor including Angkor Wat (1992) → p. 184

China:
Daoist shrines and monasteries in the Wudang Mountains (1994) → pp. 190–191
Potala Palace, Jokhang Temple and Norbulingka Palace in Lhasa, Tibet (1994) → p. 182

India:
Mahabodhi Temple in Bodh Gaya (2002) → p. 174

Japan:
Holy sites and pilgrims' routes in the Kii Mountains including Koya-san Mountain with monastery and Kukai mausoleum (2004) → p. 186

Syria:
Krak des Chevaliers (2006) → p. 73

---

* The dates in brackets are the year of inclusion in the UNESCO list. The page numbers refer to monastery illustrations in the book.

Further Reading

Benz, Ernst. *The Eastern Orthodox Church: Its Thought and Life.* New York: Doubleday/Anchor, 1963.

Brumfeld, William. *Gold in Azure. One Thousand Years of Russian Architecture.* Boston: David R Godine, 1983.

Clermont, Lothar. *Jainism and the Temples of Mount Abu und Ranakpur.* New Delhi: Prakash Books, 1998.

Curzon, Robert. *Ancient Monasteries of the East.* Piscataway, NJ: Gorgias Press, 2001.

Fischer-Schreiber, Ingrid, et al. *Rider Encyclopedia of Eastern Philosophy & Religion: Buddhism, Taoism, Zen, Hinduism.* London: Rider, 1989.

Frank, Karl Suso. *With Greater Liberty: A Short History of Christian Monasticism and Religious Orders.* Michigan: Cistercian Publications, 1993.

Frye, Timothy (ed). *The Rule of Saint Benedict.* New York: Vintage, 1998.

Gabra, Gawdat. *Coptic Monasteries: Egypt's Monastic Art and Architecture.* Cairo, New York: American University in Cairo Press, 2004.

Greene, Patrick. *Medieval Monasteries.* London: Continuum, 2005.

Hattstein, Markus and Delius, Peter (eds.). *Islam—Art and Architecture.* Königswinter: Ullmann, 2008.

Hattstein, Markus. *The Story of World Religions.* Königswinter: Ullmann, 2008.

Iogna-Prat, Dominique. *Order and Exclusion: Cluny and Christendom Face Heresy, Judaism and Islam (1000–1150).* Ithaca, NY: Cornell University Press, 2002.

Keevill, Graham, Aston, Mick and Hall, Teresa. *Monastic Archaeology.* Oxford: Oxbow, 2001.

King, Peter. *Western Monasticism: A History of the Monastic Movement in the Latin Church.* Michigan: Cistercian Publications, 2000.

Knowles, David. *Christian Monasticism.* London: Weidenfeld & Nicolson, 1969.

Lawrence, C.H. *Medieval Monasticism: Forms of Religious Life in Western Europe in the Middle Ages.* Harlow: Longman, 2001.

Le Goff, Jacques. *Saint Francis of Assisi.* London: Routledge, 2004.

Leroux-Dhuys, Jean-François. *Cistercian Abbeys: History and Architecture.* Königswinter: Ullmann, 2008.

Leroy, J. *Monks and Monasteries of the Near East.* Piscataway, NJ: Gorgias Press, 2004.

Luxford, Julian M. *The Art and Architecture of English Benedictine Monasteries, 1300–1540.* Woodbridge: Boydell & Brewer, 2005.

Matarasso, Pauline M. *The Cistercian World: Monastic Writings of the Twelfth Century.* London: Penguin, 1993.

Michell, George. *The Hindu Temple. An Introduction to its Meanings and Forms.* Chicago: University of Chicago Press, 1988.

Mottola, Anthony. *Spiritual Exercises of Saint Ignatius.* New York: Image, 1964.

Mullett, Margaret. *Founders and Refounders of Byzantine Monasteries.* Belfast: Queen's University of Belfast, 2007.

Nees, Lawrence. *Early Medieval Art.* Oxford: Oxford University Press, 2002.

O'Malley, John W. *The First Jesuits.* Cambridge, MA: Harvard University Press, 1995.

Ozment, Steven. *The Age of Reform: 1250–1550. An Intellectual and Religious History of Late Medieval and Reformation Europe.* New Haven: Yale University Press, 1981.

Pevsner, Nikolaus, Fleming, John and Honour, Hugh (eds.). *The Penguin Dictionary of Architecture and Landscape Architecture.* London: Penguin, 2000.

Qiao, Yun. *Taoist Buildings.* New York: Springer, 2001.

Rajesh, M. N. *Sacred Sites: The Buddhist Monastery.* New Delhi: Roli Books, 1999.

Robinet, Isabelle. *Taoism: Growth of a Religion.* Stanford: Stanford University Press, 1997.

Schütz, Bernhard. *Great Monasteries of Europe.* New York: Abbeville Press, 2004.

Southern, R.W. *Western Society and the Church in the Middle Ages.* London: Penguin, 1990.

Uhlfelder, Myra L. (trans.). *The Dialogues of Gregory the Great. Book II. Saint Benedict.* Indianapolis: Bobbs-Merrill, 1967.

Vyuer, Jane M. De. *The Artistic Unity of the Russian Orthodox Church.* Michigan: Firebird, 2002.

Warland, Rainer, Kruger, Kristina and Toman, Rolf. *Monasteries and Monastic Orders.* Königswinter: Ullmann, 2008.

Watson, John H. *Among the Copts.* Brighton: Sussex Academic Press, 2000.

Index

Picture Credits

Frontispiece (p. 2):
*View looking west of the interior of the **Upper Church of San Francesco at Assisi**, showing the decorative ceiling and filigree rose window above the entrance.*

This is a Parragon Publishing Book

This edition published in 2011

Parragon Publishing
Queen Street House
4 Queen Street
Bath BA1 1HE, UK

English-language edition produced by Cambridge Publishing Management Ltd
Project editor: Frances Darby
Translator: Richard Elliott
Copy editor: Penny Isaac
Typesetter: Donna Pedley
Proofreader: Beth Beemer
Indexer: Marie Lorimer

ISBN: 978-1-4454-2859-8

Printed in Malaysia